From

_____

Date

_____

_____

# God's simple solutions

## 12 biblical principles for better health

*The quoted ideas expressed in this book (but not Scripture verses) are not, in all cases, exact quotations, as some have been edited for clarity and brevity. In all cases, the author has attempted to maintain the speaker's original intent. In some cases, quoted material for this book was obtained from secondary sources, primarily print media. While every effort was made to ensure the accuracy of these sources, the accuracy cannot be guaranteed. For additions, deletions, corrections, or clarifications in future editions of this text, please write Freeman-Smith, LLC.*

The Holy Bible, King James Version

The Holy Bible, New King James Version (NKJV) Copyright © 1982 by Thomas Nelson, Inc. Used by permission.

The Holman Christian Standard Bible™ (HCSB) Copyright © 1999, 2000, 2001 by Holman Bible Publishers. Used by permission.

The Holy Bible, New International Version®. (NIV) Copyright © 1973, 1978, 1984 International Bible Society. Used by permission of Zondervan. All rights reserved.

The Holy Bible. New Living Translation (NLT) copyright © 1996 Tyndale Charitable Trust. Used by permission of Tyndale House Publishers.

Scripture taken from The Message. (MSG) Copyright © 1993, 1994, 1995, 1996, 2000, 2001, 2002. Used by permission of NavPress Publishing Group.

International Children's Bible®, New Century Version®. (ICB) Copyright © 1986, 1988, 1999 by Tommy Nelson™, a division of Thomas Nelson, Inc. All rights reserved. Used by permission.

The New American Standard Bible®, (NASB) Copyright © 1960, 1962, 1963, 1968, 1971, 1972, 1973, 1975, 1977, 1995 by The Lockman Foundation. Used by permission.

New Century Version®. (NCV) Copyright © 1987, 1988, 1991 by Word Publishing, a division of Thomas Nelson, Inc. All rights reserved. Used by permission.

Cover Design by Kim Russell / Wahoo Designs
Page Layout by Bart Dawson

ISBN 978-1-60587-205-6

Printed in the United States of America

# God's simple solutions

## 12 biblical principles for better health

# Table of Contents

# A Message to Readers

The advice in this book is general in nature, and your circumstances are specific to you. For that reason, we strongly suggest that you consult your physician before beginning any new regimen of physical exercise or diet. Don't depend upon this book—or any other book like it—to be your sole source of information on matters pertaining to your health. Instead, consider Proverbs 1:5 and seek wise counsel from a variety of sources, especially your personal physician, before making major health-related decisions.

# Introduction

Countless books have been written on the topics of health and fitness. But if you're a Christian, you probably already own at least one copy—and more likely several copies—of the world's foremost guide to spiritual, physical, and emotional health. That book is the Holy Bible. The Bible is the irreplaceable guidebook for faithful believers—like you—who seek God's wisdom and His truth.

God has a plan for every aspect of your life, including your health. But God will not force His plans upon you; to the contrary, He has given you the ability to make choices. The consequences of those choices help determine the quality and the tone of your life. This book is intended to help you make wise choices—choices that will lead to spiritual, physical, and emotional fitness—by encouraging you to rely upon a dozen simple principles found in God's Holy Word.

Health is a gift from God. What we do with that gift is determined, to a surprising extent, by the person we see every time we gaze into the mirror. If we squander our health—or if we take it for granted—we do a profound disservice to ourselves and to our loved ones. But God has other plans. He commands us to treat our bodies, our minds, and our souls with the utmost care. And that's exactly what we should do.

If you seek to protect and to enhance your spiritual, emotional, and physical health, these pages will help, but they offer no shortcuts. Healthy living is a journey, not a destination, and that journey requires discipline. If you're willing to make the step-by-step journey toward improved health, rest assured that God is taking careful note of your progress . . . and He's quietly urging you to take the next step.

# Principle 1

# God Has a Plan for Your Health

*Who is the person who fears the Lord?*
*He will show him the way he should choose.*
*He will live a good life, and his descendants will inherit the land.*
Psalm 25:12-13 HCSB

The journey toward improved health is not only a common-sense exercise in personal discipline, it is also a spiritual journey ordained by our Creator. God does not intend that we abuse our bodies by giving in to excessive appetites or to slothful behavior. To the contrary, God has instructed us to protect our physical bodies to the greatest extent we can. To do otherwise is to disobey Him.

When you make the decision to seek God's will for your life—and you should—then you will contemplate His Word, and you will be watchful for His signs. God intends to use you in wonderful, unexpected ways if you let Him. But be forewarned: the decision to seek God's plan and fulfill His purpose is ultimately a decision that you must make by yourself and for yourself. The consequences of that decision have implications that are both profound and eternal, so choose carefully. And then, as you go about your daily activities, keep your eyes and ears open, as well as your heart, because God is patiently trying to get His message through . . . and there's no better moment than this one for you to help Him.

**Remember This:**
God has a plan for your spiritual, physical, and emotional health.

## More from God's Word

*We know that all things work together for the good of those who love God: those who are called according to His purpose.*

Romans 8:28 HCSB

*The steps of the Godly are directed by the Lord. He delights in every detail of their lives. Though they stumble, they will not fall, for the Lord holds them by the hand.*

Psalm 37:23-24 NLT

*For it is God who is working among you both the willing and the working for His good purpose.*

Philippians 2:13 HCSB

*The Lord says, "I will make you wise and show you where to go. I will guide you and watch over you."*

Psalm 32:8 NCV

*Lord, You light my lamp; my God illuminates my darkness.*

Psalm 18:28 HCSB

## More Thoughts About God's Plan

It's incredible to realize that what we do each day has meaning in the big picture of God's plan.

Bill Hybels

When the dream of our heart is one that God has planted there, a strange happiness flows into us. At that moment, all of the spiritual resources of the universe are released to help us. Our praying is then at one with the will of God and becomes a channel for the Creator's purposes for us and our world.

Catherine Marshall

God's all-sufficiency is a major. Your inability is a minor. Major in majors, not in minors.

Corrie ten Boom

## Just Say No to Junk Food

We live in a junk-food society, but you shouldn't let your house become junk-food heaven. Make your home a haven of healthy foods. And remember, it's never too soon to teach your kids good habits . . . and that includes the very good habit of sensible eating.

# Actions Reflect Beliefs

English clergyman Thomas Fuller observed, "He does not believe who does not live according to his beliefs." These words are most certainly true. We may proclaim our beliefs to our hearts' content, but our proclamations will mean nothing—to others or to ourselves—unless we accompany our words with deeds that match. The sermons that we live are far more compelling than the ones we preach.

Like it or not, your life is an accurate reflection of your creed. If this fact gives you some cause for concern, don't bother talking about the changes that you intend to make— make them. And then, when your good deeds speak for themselves—as they most certainly will—don't interrupt.

### It's Part of God's Plan for You

Do you think God wants you to develop healthy habits? Of course He does! Physical, emotional, and spiritual fitness are all part of God's plan for you. But it's up to you to make certain that a healthy lifestyle is a fundamental part of your plan, too.

God has a plan for the life of
every Christian. Every circumstance,
every turn of destiny,
all things work together for
your good and for His glory.

—

Billy Graham

# Doing Things His Way

D o you want to experience a life filled with abundance and peace? If so, here's a word of warning: you'll need to resist the temptation to do things "your way" and you must commit, instead, to do things God's way.

Just for the record, here are the facts: 1. God has plans for your life that are far grander than you can imagine. 2. It's up to you to discover those plans and accomplish them . . . or not.

Sometimes, God's plans are crystal clear, but other times, He may lead you through the wilderness before He delivers you to the Promised Land. So be patient, keep praying, and keep seeking His will for your life. When you do, you'll be amazed at the marvelous things that an all-powerful, all-knowing God can do.

## Follow His Lead

God has a plan for the world and for you. When you discover His plan for your life—and when you follow in the footsteps of His Son—you will be rewarded. The place where God is leading you is the place where you must go.

## More from God's Word About Values

*God's Way is not a matter of mere talk; it's an empowered life.*

1 Corinthians 4:20 MSG

*We encouraged, comforted, and implored each one of you to walk worthy of God, who calls you into His own kingdom and glory.*

1 Thessalonians 2:12 HCSB

*Therefore, since we have this ministry, as we have received mercy, we do not give up. Instead, we have renounced shameful secret things, not walking in deceit or distorting God's message, but in God's sight we commend ourselves to every person's conscience by an open display of the truth.*

2 Corinthians 4:1-2 HCSB

*So we must not get tired of doing good, for we will reap at the proper time if we don't give up.*

Galatians 6:9 HCSB

*Blessed are those who hunger and thirst for righteousness, because they will be filled.*

Matthew 5:6 HCSB

# Your Partnership with God

*So now we can rejoice in our wonderful new relationship*
*with God—all because of what our Lord Jesus Christ*
*has done for us in making us friends of God.*

Romans 5:11 NLT

Physical fitness, like every other aspect of your life, begins and ends with God. If you'd like to adopt a healthier lifestyle, God is willing to help. In fact, if you sincerely wish to create a healthier you—either physically, emotionally, or spiritually—God is anxious to be your silent partner in that endeavor, but it's up to you to ask for His help.

God has a plan for every facet of your life, and His plan includes provisions for your spiritual, physical, and emotional health. But, He expects you to do your fair share of the work! In a world that is chock-full of tasty temptations, you may find it all too easy to make unhealthy choices. Your challenge, of course, is to resist those unhealthy choices by every means you can, including prayer. And you can be sure that whenever you ask for God's help, He will give it.

Our world is teeming with temptations and distractions that can rob you of the physical, emotional, and spiritual fitness that might otherwise be yours. And if you're not careful, the struggles and stresses of everyday living can rob you of the

peace that should rightfully be yours because of your personal relationship with Christ. So take time each day to have a
personal training session with your Savior. Don't be a person
who's satisfied with occasional visits to church on Sunday
morning; build a relationship with Jesus that deepens day
by day. When you do, you will most certainly encounter the
subtle hand of the Father. Then, if you are wise, you will take
His hand and follow God as He leads you on the path to a
healthier, happier life.

**Remember This:**
Your journey toward improved health can be, and should
be, a journey that you make with God.

## More from God's Word

*Don't you know that you are God's sanctuary and that the Spirit of God lives in you?*

1 Corinthians 3:16 HCSB

*Now the God of all grace, who called you to His eternal glory in Christ Jesus, will personally restore, establish, strengthen, and support you.*

1 Peter 5:10 HCSB

*Peace, peace to you, and peace to your helpers! For your God helps you.*

1 Chronicles 12:18 NKJV

*For I am persuaded that neither death nor life, nor angels nor rulers, nor things present, nor things to come, nor powers, nor height, nor depth, nor any other created thing will have the power to separate us from the love of God that is in Christ Jesus our Lord!*

Romans 8:38-39 HCSB

## More Thoughts About God's Support

Faith is not merely you holding on to God—it is God holding on to you.

E. Stanley Jones

The Rock of Ages is the great sheltering encirclement.

Oswald Chambers

We are never out of reach of Satan's devices, so we must never be without the whole armor of God.

Warren Wiersbe

As sure as God puts his children in the furnace, he will be in the furnace with them.

C. H. Spurgeon

## Start Slowly and Use Common Sense

Adopt healthy habits you can stick with. In other words, don't starve yourself. And if you're beginning an exercise regimen, start slowly. Be moderate, even in your moderation.

He stands fast as your rock,
steadfast as your safeguard,
sleepless as your watcher,
valiant as your champion.

—

C. H. Spurgeon

# Say No to Unhealthy Foods

E ating unhealthy foods is habit-forming. And if you have acquired the unfortunate habit of eating unhealthy foods, then God wants you to start making changes today.

Take a few minutes to think about your eating habits. Do you gobble down snack foods while watching television? If so, stop. Do you drink high-calorie soft drinks or feast on unhealthy snacks like potato chips or candy? If so, you're doing yourself a disservice. Do you delight in high-fat, high-calorie foods that taste good for a few seconds but accumulate on your waistlines for years? Do you load up your plate until food falls off the edge? And then do you feel obligated to eat every last bite? If so, it's time to think long and hard about the serious consequences of indulging in such unhealthy habits.

Poor eating habits are easy to make and hard to break, but break them you must. Otherwise, you'll be disobeying God's commandments while causing yourself great harm.

Maintaining a healthy lifestyle is a journey, not a destination, and that journey requires discipline. But rest assured that if you and your loved ones are willing to make the step-by-step journey toward a healthier diet, God is taking careful note of your progress . . . and He's quietly urging you to take the next step.

# God's Protection

In a world filled with dangers and temptations, God is the ultimate armor. In a world filled with misleading messages, God's Word is the ultimate truth. In a world filled with more frustrations than we can count, God's Son offers the ultimate peace. Will you accept God's peace and wear God's armor against the dangers of our world?

Sometimes, in the crush of everyday life, God may seem far away, but He is not. God is everywhere you have ever been and everywhere you will ever go. He is with you night and day; He knows your thoughts and your prayers. He is your ultimate Protector. And, when you earnestly seek His protection, you will find it because He is here—always—waiting patiently for you to reach out to Him.

## It's Up to You

The benefits of exercise are both both physical and emotional. But no one can exercise for you; it's up to you to exercise, or not.

## More from God's Word About God's Love

*For God loved the world in this way: He gave His only Son, so that everyone who believes in Him will not perish but have eternal life.*

John 3:16 HCSB

*For the Lord is good, and His love is eternal; His faithfulness endures through all generations.*

Psalm 100:5 HCSB

*The one who has My commandments and keeps them is the one who loves Me. And the one who loves Me will be loved by My Father. I also will love him and will reveal Myself to him.*

John 14:21 HCSB

*We love Him because He first loved us.*

1 John 4:19 NKJV

## It's the Best-Selling Book of All Time for a Reason.

Ruth Bell Graham, wife of evangelist Billy Graham, observed: "The Reference Point for the Christian is the Bible. All values, judgments, and attitudes must be gauged in relationship to this Reference Point." Make certain that you're an avid reader of God's best seller, and make sure that you keep reading it as long as you live!

*Draw near to God,
and He will draw near to you.*

—

James 4:8 HCSB

## Notes to Yourself

In the space below, write down some of the health-related steps that you think God wants you to take today, this week, and this year.

_____

_____

_____

_____

_____

_____

_____

_____

_____

_____

_____

_____

_____

# Your Body Is God's Temple, and He Expects You to Take Care of It

*Therefore, brothers, by the mercies of God,*
*I urge you to present your bodies as a living sacrifice,*
*holy and pleasing to God; this is your spiritual worship.*
Romans 12:1 HCSB

I n the 12th chapter of Romans, Paul encourages us to make our bodies "holy and pleasing to God." Paul adds that to do so is a "spiritual act of worship." For believers, the implication is clear: God intends that we take special care of the bodies He has given us. But it's tempting to do otherwise.

We live in a fast-food world where unhealthy choices are convenient, inexpensive, and tempting. And, we live in a digital world filled with modern conveniences that often rob us of the physical exercise needed to maintain healthy lifestyles. As a result, too many of us find ourselves glued to the television, with a snack in one hand and a clicker in the other. The results are as unfortunate as they are predictable.

How do you treat your body? Do you treat it with the reverence and respect it deserves, or do you take it more or less for granted? Well, the Bible has clear instructions about the way you should take care of the miraculous body that God has given you.

God's Word teaches us that our bodies are "temples" that belong to God (1 Corinthians 6:19-20). We are commanded (not encouraged, not advised—we are commanded!) to treat our bodies with respect and honor. We do so by making wise choices and by making those choices consistently over an extended period of time.

## More from God's Word

*Don't you know that you are God's sanctuary and that the Spirit of God lives in you?*

1 Corinthians 3:16 HCSB

*For we know that if our earthly house, a tent, is destroyed, we have a building from God, a house not made with hands, eternal in the heavens.*

2 Corinthians 5:1 HCSB

*For it was You who created my inward parts; You knit me together in my mother's womb. I will praise You, because I have been remarkably and wonderfully made.*

Psalm 139:13-14 HCSB

### Remember This:
If you're not determined to be the master of your body
. . . then you might just become a slave to your impulses.

## More Thoughts About Taking Care of Your Body

Our body is like armor, our soul like the warrior. Take care of both, and you will be ready for what comes.

Amma St. Syncletice

Food ought to be a refreshment to the body, and not a burden.

St. Bonaventure

Eat to live, and not live to eat.

Poor Richard's Almanac

In general, mankind, since the improvement of cookery, eats twice as much as nature requires.

Ben Franklin

## Become an Educated Consumer

Educate yourself on which foods are healthy and which foods aren't. Read labels and learn the basics of proper nutrition. Then, use common sense and discipline in planning your diet.

# What Kind of Eater Are You?

Take a few minutes to examine your eating habits. Do you gobble down snack foods while watching television? If so, stop. Do you drink high-calorie soft drinks or feast on unhealthy snacks like potato chips or candy? If so, you're doing yourself a disservice? Do you load up your plate and then feel obligated to eat every last bite? If so, it's time to form some new habits.

Poor eating habits are usually well established, so they won't be easy to change, but change them you must if you want to enjoy the benefits of a healthy lifestyle.

### When It Comes to Exercise, Persistence Pays

An exercise program that starts slowly and builds over time is far better than an exercise program that starts—and ends—quickly.

# Making the Right Choices

Life is a series of choices. Each day, we make countless decisions that can bring us closer to God . . . or not. When we live according to God's commandments, we earn for ourselves the abundance and peace that He intends for us to experience. But, when we turn our backs upon God by disobeying Him, we bring needless suffering upon ourselves and our families.

Do you seek God's peace and His blessings? Then obey Him. When you're faced with a difficult choice or a powerful temptation, seek God's counsel and trust the counsel He gives. Invite God into your heart and live according to His commandments. When you do, you will be blessed today, tomorrow, and forever.

God has given you a guidebook for righteous living called the Holy Bible. It contains thorough instructions which, if followed, lead to fulfillment and salvation. But, if you choose to ignore God's commandments, the results are as predictable as they are tragic.

So here's a surefire formula for a happy, abundant life: live righteously. And for further instructions, read the manual.

## More from God's Word About Righteousness

*The righteous one will live by his faith.*

Habakkuk 2:4 HCSB

*And the world is passing away, and the lust of it; but he who does the will of God abides forever.*

1 John 2:17 NKJV

*Because the eyes of the Lord are on the righteous and His ears are open to their request. But the face of the Lord is against those who do evil.*

1 Peter 3:12 HCSB

*Flee from youthful passions, and pursue righteousness, faith, love, and peace, along with those who call on the Lord from a pure heart.*

2 Timothy 2:22 HCSB

## Have Faith and Get Busy

Here's a time-tested formula for success: have faith in God and do the work. It has been said that there are no shortcuts to any place worth going, and those words apply to your physical fitness, too. There are simply no shortcuts to a healthy lifestyle.

# To Improve Your Health, Improve Your Habits

*A prudent person foresees the danger ahead and takes precautions.*
*The simpleton goes blindly on and suffers the consequences.*
Proverbs 27:12 NLT

If you're like most people, you've already tried, perhaps on many occasions, to form healthier habits. You've employed your own willpower in a noble effort to create a new, improved, healthier you. You've probably tried to improve various aspects of your spiritual, physical, or emotional health. Perhaps you've gone on diets, or made New Year's resolutions, or tried the latest self-help fad in an attempt to finally make important changes in your life. And if you're like most people, you've been successful . . . for a while. But eventually, those old familiar habits came creeping back into your life, and the improvements that you had made proved to be temporary.

If you'd like to improve your physical or emotional health, try this: Depend less upon your own willpower and more upon God's infinite power.

Whenever your own willpower begins to weaken, turn to God in prayer. Then, as you establish a true partnership with the Creator, you'll quickly discover that there's no limit to the things that the two of you, working together, can accomplish.

**Remember This:**

When you form a deeper relationship with God, you can start establishing healthier habits, starting now.

## More from God's Word

*Dear friend, I pray that you may prosper in every way and be in good health, just as your soul prospers.*

3 John 1:2 HCSB

*Do you not know that your body is a sanctuary of the Holy Spirit who is in you, whom you have from God? You are not your own, for you were bought at a price; therefore glorify God in your body.*

1 Corinthians 6:19-20 HCSB

*Guard your heart above all else, for it is the source of life.*

Proverbs 4:23 HCSB

*Acquire wisdom—how much better it is than gold! And acquire understanding—it is preferable to silver.*

Proverbs 16:16 HCSB

*Therefore, everyone who hears these words of Mine and acts on them will be like a sensible man who built his house on the rock. The rain fell, the rivers rose, and the winds blew and pounded that house. Yet it didn't collapse, because its foundation was on the rock.*

Matthew 7:24–25 HCSB

## More Thoughts About Your Habits

You will never change your life until you change something you do daily.

John Maxwell

Begin to be now what you will be hereafter.

St. Jerome

If you want to form a new habit, get to work. If you want to break a bad habit, get on your knees.

Marie T. Freeman

## Very Big Portions Make Very Little Sense

Do you dine out often? If so, be careful. Most restaurants stay in business by serving big portions of tasty food. Unfortunately, most restaurant food is high in calories, sugar, and fat. You will probably eat healthier meals if you prepare those meals at home instead of eating out.

You can build up a set
of good habits so that you habitually
take the Christian way
without thought.

—

E. Stanley Jones

# Forming Healthy Habits

I t's an old saying and a true one: First, you make your habits, and then your habits make you. Some habits will inevitably bring you closer to God; other habits will lead you away from the path He has chosen for you. If you sincerely desire to improve your spiritual health, you must honestly examine the habits that make up the fabric of your day. And you must abandon those habits that are displeasing to God.

If you trust God, and if you keep asking for His help, He can transform your life. If you sincerely ask Him to help you, the same God who created the universe will help you defeat the harmful habits that have heretofore defeated you. So, if at first you don't succeed, keep praying. God is listening, and He's ready to help you become a better person if you ask Him . . . so ask today.

### Integrating God's Word into Your Life

Perhaps you have tended to divide the concerns of your life into two categories: "spiritual" and "other." If so, it's time to reconsider. God intends you to integrate His commandments into every aspect of your life, and that includes your physical and emotional health, too.

# Moving Mountains

Every life—including yours—is a series of successes and failures, celebrations and disappointments, joys and sorrows. Every step of the way, through every triumph and tragedy, God will stand by your side and strengthen you . . . if you have faith in Him. Jesus taught His disciples that if they had faith, they could move mountains. You can too.

When a suffering woman sought healing by merely touching the hem of His cloak, Jesus replied, "Daughter, be of good comfort; thy faith hath made thee whole" (Matthew 9:22 KJV). The message to believers of every generation is clear: we must live by faith today and every day.

When you place your faith, your trust, indeed your life in the hands of Christ Jesus, you'll be amazed at the marvelous things He can do with you and through you. So strengthen your faith through praise, through worship, through Bible study, and through prayer. And trust God's plans. With Him, all things are possible, and He stands ready to open a world of possibilities to you . . . if you have faith.

**Talk to Your Doctor About Exercise**

Before you begin a major new exercise program, see your doctor: As the old saying goes, it's better to be safe than sorry.

## More from God's Word About Faith

*If you do not stand firm in your faith, then you will not stand at all.*

Isaiah 7:9 HCSB

*Be alert, stand firm in the faith, be brave and strong.*

1 Corinthians 16:13 HCSB

*For we walk by faith, not by sight.*

2 Corinthians 5:7 HCSB

*Now faith is the reality of what is hoped for, the proof of what is not seen.*

Hebrews 11:1 HCSB

*Now without faith it is impossible to please God, for the one who draws near to Him must believe that He exists and rewards those who seek Him.*

Hebrews 11:6 HCSB

## Notes to Yourself

In the space below, make notes about the healthy habits that you'd like to establish. Then, make notes about the unhealthy habits you'd like to change.

_____

_____

_____

_____

_____

_____

_____

_____

_____

_____

_____

_____

_____

_____

# Principle 3

# When You Ask God for His Help, He Will Give It

*So I say to you, ask, and it will be given to you; seek,*
*and you will find; knock, and it will be opened to you.*
*For everyone who asks receives, and he who seeks finds,*
*and to him who knocks it will be opened.*
Luke 11:9-10 NKJV

D o you genuinely want to strengthen your fitness and your faith? If the answer to that question is yes, then you should set aside ample time each morning to ask for God's help.

Is prayer an integral part of your daily life, or is it a hit-or-miss habit? Do you "pray without ceasing," or is your prayer life an afterthought? Do you regularly pray in the quiet moments of the early morning, or do you bow your head only when others are watching?

As Christians, we are instructed to pray often. But it is important to note that genuine prayer requires much more than bending our knees and closing our eyes. Heartfelt prayer is an attitude of the heart.

If your prayers have become more a matter of habit than a matter of passion, you're robbing yourself of a deeper relationship with God. And how can you rectify that situation? By praying more frequently and more fervently. When you do, God will shower you with His blessings, His grace, and His love.

Too many of us, even well-intentioned believers, tend to "compartmentalize" our waking hours into a few familiar categories: work, rest, play, family time, and worship. To do so is a mistake. Worship and praise should be woven into the fabric of our lives; prayer should never be relegated to a weekly three-hour visit to church on Sunday morning.

Theologian Wayne Oates once admitted, "Many of my prayers are made with my eyes open. You see, it seems I'm always praying about something, and it's not always convenient—or safe—to close my eyes." Dr. Oates understood that God always hears our prayers and that the relative position of our eyelids is of no concern to Him.

Today, find a little more time to lift your concerns to God in prayer, and praise Him for all that He has done. He's listening . . . and He wants to hear from you.

### Remember This:
If you're serious about improving your fitness or your faith, pray about it.

## More from God's Word

*The intense prayer of the righteous is very powerful.*

James 5:16 HCSB

*Let the words of my mouth and the meditation of my heart be acceptable in Your sight, O Lord, my strength and my Redeemer.*

Psalm 19:14 NKJV

*Yet He often withdrew to deserted places and prayed.*

Luke 5:16 HCSB

*Rejoice in hope; be patient in affliction; be persistent in prayer.*

Romans 12:12 HCSB

*Is anyone among you suffering? He should pray. Is anyone cheerful? He should sing praises.*

James 5:13 HCSB

## More Thoughts About the Power of Prayer

A life growing in its purity and devotion will be a more prayerful life.

E. M. Bounds

God knows that we, with our limited vision, don't even know that for which we should pray. When we entrust our requests to him, we trust him to honor our prayers with holy judgment.

Max Lucado

When we are in the presence of God, removed from distractions, we are able to hear him more clearly, and a secure environment has been established for the young and broken places in our hearts to surface.

John Eldredge

## Pray About Your Health

As you petition God each morning, ask Him for the strength and the wisdom to treat your body as His creation and His "temple." During the day ahead, you will face countless temptations to do otherwise, but with God's help, you can treat your body as the priceless, one-of-a-kind gift that it most certainly is.

# Ask for God's Help

God wants you to experience abundant life, but He will not force you to adopt a healthy lifestyle. Managing your food and your fitness is up to you.

If you want more from life, ask more from God. D. L. Moody observed, "Some people think God does not like to be troubled with our constant asking. But, the way to trouble God is not to come at all." So, if you seek an improved level of fitness—or if you seek any other worthy goal—ask God (and keep asking Him) until He answers your prayers.

**Day In, Day Out**

Your journey with God unfolds day by day, and that's precisely how your journey to an improved state of physical fitness must also unfold: moment by moment, day by day, year by year.

# Pray Constantly

God's Word promises that prayer is a powerful tool for changing your life and your world. So here's a question: Are you using prayer as a powerful tool to improve your world, or are you praying sporadically at best? If you're wise, you've learned that prayer is indeed powerful and that it is most powerful when it is used often.

Today, if you haven't already done so, establish the habit of praying constantly. Don't pray day-to-day; pray hour-to-hour. Start each day with prayer, end it with prayer, and fill it with prayer. That's the best way to know God; it's the best way to change your world; and it is, quite simply, the best way to live.

### Ask More Frequently

If life's inevitable temptations seem to be getting the best of you, try praying more often, even if many of those prayers are simply brief, "open-eyed" requests to your Father in heaven.

## More from God's Word About Asking for God's Help

*If you remain in Me and My words remain in you, ask whatever you want and it will be done for you.*

John 15:7 HCSB

*What father among you, if his son asks for a fish, will, instead of a fish, give him a snake? Or if he asks for an egg, will give him a scorpion? If you then, who are evil, know how to give good gifts to your children, how much more will the heavenly Father give the Holy Spirit to those who ask Him?*

Luke 11:11-13 HCSB

*Don't worry about anything, but in everything, through prayer and petition with thanksgiving, let your requests be made known to God.*

Philippians 4:6 HCSB

*You do not have because you do not ask.*

James 4:2 HCSB

*For the Lord gives wisdom; from His mouth come knowledge and understanding.*

Proverbs 2:6 NKJV

# The Power of Daily Worship and Meditation

*Man shall not live by bread alone, but by every word
that proceeds from the mouth of God.*
Matthew 4:4 NKJV

Are you concerned about your spiritual, physical, or emotional fitness? If so, there is a timeless source of advice and comfort upon which you can—and should—depend. That source is the Holy Bible.

God's Word has much to say about every aspect of your life, including your health. If you face personal health challenges that seem almost insoluble, have faith and seek God's wisdom. If you can't seem to get yourself on a sensible diet or on a program of regular physical exercise, consult God's teachings. If your approach to your physical or emotional health has, up to this point, been undisciplined, pray for the strength to do what you know is right.

God has given you the Holy Bible for the purpose of knowing His promises, His power, His commandments, His wisdom, His love, and His Son. As you seek to improve the state of your own health, study God's teachings and apply them to your life. When you do, you will be blessed, now and forever.

## More from God's Word

*He awakens Me morning by morning, He awakens My ear to hear as the learned. The Lord God has opened My ear.*

Isaiah 50:4-5 NKJV

*Lord, You are my lamp; the Lord illuminates my darkness.*

2 Samuel 22:29 HCSB

*Teach me Your way, Lord, and I will live by Your truth. Give me an undivided mind to fear Your name.*

Psalm 86:11 HCSB

*Happy is the man who finds wisdom, and the man who gains understanding.*

Proverbs 3:13 NKJV

### Remember This:

God's Word has the power to change every aspect of your life, including your health.

## More Thoughts About Your Daily Devotional

We must appropriate the tender mercy of God every day after conversion or problems quickly develop. We need his grace daily in order to live a righteous life.

Jim Cymbala

Make a plan now to keep a daily appointment with God. The enemy is going to tell you to set it aside, but you must carve out the time. If you're too busy to meet with the Lord, friend, then you are simply too busy.

Charles Swindoll

I suggest you discipline yourself to spend time daily in a systematic reading of God's Word. Make this "quiet time" a priority that nobody can change.

Warren Wiersbe

## What Is Your Refrigerator Trying to Tell You?

Take a careful look inside your refrigerator. Are the contents reflective of a healthy lifestyle? And if your fridge is overflowing with junk foods, it's time to rethink your shopping habits.

# Your Fitness and Your Faith

Faith and fitness. These two words may seem disconnected, but they are not. If you're about to begin a regimen of vigorous physical exercise, then you will find it helpful to begin a regimen of vigorous spiritual exercise, too. Why? Because the physical, emotional, and spiritual aspects of your life are interconnected. In other words, you cannot "compartmentalize" physical fitness in one category of your being and spiritual fitness in another—every facet of your life has an impact on the person you are today and the person you will become tomorrow. That's why your body is so important to God—your body is, quite literally, the "temple" that houses "the Spirit of God" that dwells within you (1 Corinthians 3:16).

God's Word contains powerful lessons about every aspect of your life, including your health. So, if you're concerned about your spiritual, physical, or emotional health, the first place to turn is that timeless source of comfort and assurance, the Holy Bible. When you open your Bible and begin reading, you'll quickly be reminded of this fact: when you face concerns of any sort—including health-related challenges—God is with you. And His healing touch, like His love, endures forever.

God has given us the Bible for the purpose of knowing His promises, His power, His commandments, His wisdom,

His love, and His Son. As we study God's teachings and apply them to our lives, we live by the Word that shall never pass away. So if you're about to begin a new fitness program, be sure that you also pay careful attention to God's program by studying His Word every day of your life.

## What the Bible Says About Your Health

God's Word is full of advice about health, moderation, and sensible living. When you come across these passages, take them to heart and put them to use.

# Spending Quiet Time with God

The Bible promises that a good way to know God is to be still and listen to Him. But sometimes, you may find it hard to slow down and listen. As the demands of everyday life weigh down upon you, you may become so wrapped up in your obligations that you just don't take enough time for God. A far better strategy, of course, is to quiet yourself every day. When you do, you will experience the Father's presence and His love. Then, God will touch your heart, He will restore your spirits, and He will give you the perspective you need to make good decisions.

As you petition God each morning, ask Him for the strength and the wisdom to live moderately and wisely. Ask Him to help you treat your body as His temple. During the day ahead, you will face countless temptations to do otherwise, but with God's help, you can treat your body as the priceless, one-of-a-kind gift that it most certainly is.

### Studying the Bible Is Not Enough

Your daily devotional should have a major impact on your day. Don't just study the Bible; live by it!

## More from God's Word About Silence

*Be still, and know that I am God.*

Psalm 46:10 NKJV

*Be silent before the Lord and wait expectantly for Him.*

Psalm 37:7 HCSB

*In quietness and confidence shall be your strength.*

Isaiah 30:15 NKJV

*I am not alone, because the Father is with Me.*

John 16:32 HCSB

*Draw near to God, and He will draw near to you.*

James 4:8 HCSB

## Notes to Yourself

In the space below, write down some of the benefits that you earn whenever you start your day with God.

_____

_____

_____

_____

_____

_____

_____

_____

_____

_____

_____

_____

_____

# Principle 4

# God Can Help You Bring Balance to Your Life

*Come to Me, all you who labor and are heavy laden,*
*and I will give you rest. Take My yoke upon you and learn from*
*Me, for I am gentle and lowly in heart, and you will find rest for*
*your souls. For My yoke is easy and My burden is light.*
Matthew 11:28-30 NKJV

Sometimes, amid the demands of daily life, we lose perspective. Life seems out of balance, and the pressures of everyday living seem overwhelming. What's needed is a fresh perspective, a restored sense of balance...and God.

If a temporary loss of perspective has robbed you of the spiritual fitness that should be yours in Christ, it's time to readjust your thought patterns. Negative thoughts are habit-forming; thankfully, so are positive ones. With practice, you can form the habit of focusing on God's priorities and your possibilities. When you do, you'll soon discover that you will spend less time fretting about your challenges and more time praising God for His gifts.

When you call upon the Lord and prayerfully seek His will, He will give you wisdom and perspective. When you make God's priorities your priorities, He will direct your steps and calm your fears. So today and every day hereafter, pray for a sense of balance and perspective. And remember: your thoughts are intensely powerful things, so handle them with care.

### Remember This:

Life is a balancing act. To improve your balance, consult your heavenly Father many times each day.

## More from God's Word

*Finally brothers, whatever is true, whatever is honorable, whatever is just, whatever is pure, whatever is lovely, whatever is commendable— if there is any moral excellence and if there is any praise—dwell on these things.*

Philippians 4:8 HCSB

*It is better to get wisdom than gold, and to choose understanding rather than silver!*

Proverbs 16:16 NCV

*People's thoughts can be like a deep well, but someone with understanding can find the wisdom there.*

Proverbs 20:5 NCV

*Don't copy the behavior and customs of this world, but let God transform you into a new person by changing the way you think. Then you will know what God wants you to do, and you will know how good and pleasing and perfect his will really is.*

Romans 12:2 NLT

## More Thoughts About Balance

Prescription for a happier and healthier life: resolve to slow down your pace; learn to say no gracefully; resist the temptation to chase after more pleasure, more hobbies, and more social entanglements.

*James Dobson*

Notice what Jesus had to say concerning those who have wearied themselves by trying to do things in their own strength: "Come to me, all you who labor and are heavy laden, and I will give you rest."

*Henry Blackaby and Claude King*

Jesus gives us the ultimate rest, the confidence we need, to escape the frustration and chaos of the world around us.

*Billy Graham*

## It's Up to You

Simply put, it's up to you to assume the ultimate responsibility for your health. So if you're fighting the battle of the bulge (the bulging waistline, that is), don't waste your time blaming the fast food industry—or anybody else, for that matter. It's your body, and it's your responsibility to take care of it.

# Finding Time for Recreation

Are you one of those people who seldom takes a day off? Are you a seven-day-a-week worker bee, or a closet workaholic? If so, it's time to reorder your priorities. Why? Because an essential element of physical, emotional, and spiritual fitness is simply this: the ability to relax and enjoy leisure time.

The words of Psalm 118:24 remind us of a profound yet simple truth: "This is the day the LORD has made; let us rejoice and be glad in it" (NIV). Yet we may find ourselves so wrapped up in the demands of everyday living that we forget to celebrate God's glorious gift. That's a BIG mistake.

Are you willing to relax long enough so that you can celebrate this glorious day with your family and friends? Hopefully so, because this day is a one-of-a-kind treasure that can—and should—be a cause for joyful celebration. Part of that celebration means finding an appropriate balance between work and play.

## Little Decisions Add Up

When taken together over a long period of time, little decisions can have big consequences. So remember: when it comes to matters of health and fitness, there are no "small" decisions.

# Peace and Renewal

One aspect of spiritual health is the ability to partake in the peace that only God can give. Are you willing to accept God's peace? If you can genuinely answer that question with a resounding yes, then you are richly blessed. But if you have not yet discovered "the peace that passes all understanding," today is a wonderful day to find it.

The beautiful words of John 14:27 give us hope: "Peace I leave with you, my peace I give to you . . . ." Jesus offers us peace, not as the world gives, but as He alone gives. We, as believers, can accept His peace or ignore it.

When we accept the peace of Jesus Christ into our hearts, our lives are transformed. And then, because we possess the gift of peace, we can share that gift with fellow Christians, family members, friends, and associates. If, on the other hand, we choose to ignore the gift of peace—for whatever reason—we simply cannot share what we do not possess.

Today, as a gift to yourself, to your family, and to your friends, make peace with the past by forgiving those who have harmed you. Then, claim the inner peace that is your spiritual birthright: the peace of Jesus Christ. It is offered freely; it has been paid for in full; it is yours for the asking. So ask. And then share.

## More from God's Word About God's Faithfulness

*I will sing of the tender mercies of the Lord forever! Young and old will hear of your faithfulness. Your unfailing love will last forever. Your faithfulness is as enduring as the heavens.*

Psalm 89:1-2 NLT

*God is faithful, by whom you were called into the fellowship of His Son, Jesus Christ our Lord.*

1 Corinthians 1:9 NKJV

*Because of the LORD'S great love we are not consumed, for his compassions never fail. They are new every morning; great is your faithfulness.*

Lamentations 3:22-23 NIV

## Spend Time Every Day with God

Need balance? Have a daily planning session with God. A regularly scheduled time of prayer, Bible reading, and meditation can help you prioritize your day and your life. And what if you're simply too busy to spend five or ten minutes with God? If so, it's time to reorder your priorities.

# Don't Go on a Diet, Change Your Lifestyle

*Their end is destruction; their god is their stomach;*
*their glory is in their shame. They are focused on earthly things.*
Philippians 3:19 HCSB

If you want to lose weight, don't dare go on a diet! It's a sad fact, but true: in the vast majority of cases, diets simply don't work. In fact, one study that examined the results of popular diets conducted that nearly 100% of dieters suffered almost "complete relapse after 3 to 5 years." In other words, dieters almost always return to their pre-diet weights (or, in many cases, to even higher weight levels).

If diets don't work, what should you do if you weigh more than you should? The answer is straightforward: If you need to lose weight, don't start dieting; change your lifestyle.

Your current weight is the result of the number of calories that you have taken into your body versus the number of calories that you have burned. If you seek to lower your weight, then you must burn more calories (by engaging in more vigorous physical activities), or take in fewer calories (by eating more sensibly), or both. It's as simple as that.

Many of us are remarkably ill informed and amazingly apathetic about the foods we eat. We feast on high-fat fast foods. We swoon over sweets. We order up—and promptly pack away—prodigious portions. The result is a society in which too many of us become the human equivalents of the portions we purchase: oversized.

A healthier strategy, of course, is to pay more attention to the nutritional properties of our foods and less attention to their taste. But for those of us who have become accustomed to large quantities of full-flavored, high-calorie foods, old memories indeed die hard.

Should we count every calorie that we ingest from now until the day the Good Lord calls us home? Probably not. When we focus too intently upon weight reduction, we may make weight loss even harder to achieve. Instead, we should eliminate from our diets the foods that are obviously bad for us, and we should eat more of the foods that are obviously good for us. And of course, we should eat sensible amounts, not portly portions.

How hard is it for us to know the nutritional properties of the foods we eat? Not very hard. In the grocery store, almost every food item is clearly marked. In fast-food restaurants, the fat and calorie contents are posted on the wall (although the print is incredibly small, and with good reason: the health properties of these tasty tidbits are, in most cases, so poor that we should rename them "fat foods").

As informed adults, we have access to all the information that we need to make healthy dietary choices. Now it's up to each of us to make wise dietary choices, or not. Those choices are ours, and so are their consequences.

**Remember This:**

It takes wisdom to be moderate; moderation is wisdom in action.

## More from God's Word

*Do not carouse with drunkards and gluttons, for they are on their way to poverty.*

Proverbs 23:20-21 NLT

*Do you like honey? Don't eat too much of it, or it will make you sick!*

Proverbs 25:16 NLT

*Moderation is better than muscle, self-control better than political power.*

Proverbs 16:32 MSG

*Add to your faith virtue; and to virtue, knowledge; and to knowledge, temperance; and to temperance, patience; and to patience, godliness; and to godliness, brotherly kindness; and to brotherly kindness, charity.*

2 Peter 1:5-7 KJV

*Be sober! Be on the alert! Your adversary the Devil is prowling around like a roaring lion, looking for anyone he can devour.*

1 Peter 5:8 HCSB

## More Thoughts About Moderation

It's not that some people have willpower and some don't. It's that some people are ready to change and others are not.

James Gordon, M.D.

You can look at your calorie count in the same way you might look at a bank account. Every mouthful of food is a deposit and every activity that requires energy is a withdrawal. If we deposit more then we withdraw, our surplus grows larger and larger.

John Maxwell

To many, total abstinence is easier than perfect moderation.

St. Augustine

Failure is the path of least persistence.

Anonymous

## Don't Skip Meals

Are you skipping meals? Don't do it. Skipping meals isn't healthy, and it isn't a sensible way to lose weight, either.

# Moderation Leads to Abundance

I f you sincerely seek the abundant life that Christ has promised, you must learn to control your appetites before they control you. Good habits, like bad ones, are habit-forming. The sooner you acquire the habit of moderation, the better your chances for a long, happy, abundant life.

Are you running short on willpower? If so, perhaps you haven't yet asked God to give you strength. The Bible promises that God offers His power to those righteous men and women who earnestly seek it. If your willpower has failed you on numerous occasions, then it's time to turn your weaknesses over to God. If you've been having trouble standing on your own two feet, perhaps it's time to drop to your knees, in prayer.

## All Hands on Deck

If you're trying to reshape your physique or your life, don't try to do it alone. Ask for the support and encouragement of your family members and friends. You'll improve your odds of success if you enlist your own cheering section.

# Moderation Is Wisdom in Action

Moderation and wisdom are traveling companions. If we are wise, we must learn to temper our appetites, our desires, and our impulses. When we do, we are blessed, in part, because God has created a world in which temperance is rewarded and intemperance is inevitably punished.

When we allow our appetites to run wild, they usually do. When we abandon moderation, we forfeit the inner peace that God offers—but does not guarantee—to His children. When we live intemperate lives, we rob ourselves of countless blessings that would have otherwise been ours.

God's instructions are clear: if we seek to live wisely, we must be moderate in our appetites and disciplined in our behavior. To do otherwise is an affront to Him . . . and to ourselves.

### Never Stop Studying God's Word

Even if you've been studying the Bible for many years, you've still got lots to learn. Bible study should be a lifelong endeavor; make it your lifelong endeavor.

## More from God's Word About Wisdom

*Therefore, everyone who hears these words of Mine and acts on them will be like a sensible man who built his house on the rock. The rain fell, the rivers rose, and the winds blew and pounded that house. Yet it didn't collapse, because its foundation was on the rock.*

Matthew 7:24–25 HCSB

*But from Him you are in Christ Jesus, who for us became wisdom from God, as well as righteousness, sanctification, and redemption.*

1 Corinthians 1:30 HCSB

*For God has not given us a spirit of fearfulness, but one of power, love, and sound judgment.*

2 Timothy 1:7 HCSB

*Now if any of you lacks wisdom, he should ask God, who gives to all generously and without criticizing, and it will be given to him.*

James 1:5 HCSB

*But the wisdom from above is first pure, then peace-loving, gentle, compliant, full of mercy and good fruits, without favoritism and hypocrisy.*

James 3:17 HCSB

## Notes to Yourself

In the space below, make notes about aspects of your life that will be improved when you eat more moderately and exercise more regularly.

_____

_____

_____

_____

_____

_____

_____

_____

_____

_____

_____

_____

# The Best Day to Start Improving Your Health Is This Day

*Therefore, get your minds ready for action, being self-disciplined,*
*and set your hope completely on the grace to be brought*
*to you at the revelation of Jesus Christ.*
1 Peter 1:13 HCSB

I f you're determined to improve the state of your physical, spiritual, or emotional health, the best time to begin is now. But if you're like most people, you'll be tempted to put things off until tomorrow, or the next day, or the next.

The habit of putting things off until the last minute, along with its first cousin, the habit of making excuses for work that was never done, can be detrimental to your life, to your character, and to your health. Are you in the habit of doing what needs to be done when it needs to be done, or are you a dues-paying member of the Procrastinator's Club? If you're a person who has already acquired the habit of doing things sooner rather than later, congratulations! But, if you find yourself putting off all those unpleasant tasks until later, it's time to think about the consequences of your behavior.

One way that you can learn to defeat procrastination is by paying less attention to the sacrifices you're making today and more attention to the rewards you'll receive tomorrow. So, if you're trying to improve your fitness, or any other aspect of your life, don't spend endless hours fretting over your fate. Simply seek God's counsel and get busy. When you do, you will be richly rewarded because of your willingness to act.

### Remember This:
When it comes to food, fitness, or faith, the best moment to begin major improvements is the present moment.

## More from God's Word

*But be doers of the word and not hearers only.*

James 1:22 HCSB

*When you make a vow to God, don't delay fulfilling it, because He does not delight in fools. Fulfill what you vow.*

Ecclesiastes 5:4 HCSB

*For the hearers of the law are not righteous before God, but the doers of the law will be declared righteous.*

Romans 2:13 HCSB

*Well done, good and faithful servant; you were faithful over a few things, I will make you ruler over many things. Enter into the joy of your lord.*

Matthew 25:21 NKJV

*I discipline my body and bring it under strict control, so that after preaching to others, I myself will not be disqualified.*

1 Corinthians 9:27 HCSB

## More Thoughts About the Need to Take Action Now

We spend our lives dreaming of the future, not realizing that a little of it slips away every day.

Barbara Johnson

To learn new habits is everything, for it is to reach the substance of life. Life is a tissue of habits.

Henri Frédéric Amiel

Never fail to do something because you don't feel like it. Sometimes you just have to do it now, and you'll feel like it later.

Marie T. Freeman

Measure the size of the obstacles against the size of God.

Beth Moore

## Now Is the Time

Life is a gift—health must be earned. We earn good health by cultivating healthy habits. This is the right time for you to commit yourself to a more sensible lifestyle. So take a close look at your habits: how you eat, how you exercise, and how you think about your health. The only way that you'll revolutionize your physical health is to revolutionize the habits that make up the fabric of your day.

# Start Making Changes Now

Warren Wiersbe correctly observed, "A Christian should no more defile his body than a Jew would defile the temple." Unfortunately, too many of us have allowed our temples to fall into disrepair. When it comes to fitness and food, it's easy fall into bad habits. And it's easy to convince ourselves that we'll start improving our health "some day."

If we are to care for our bodies in the way that God intends, we must establish healthy habits, and we must establish them sooner rather than later.

Saint Jerome advised, "Begin to be now what you will be hereafter." You should take his advice seriously, and you should take it NOW. When it comes to your health, it's always the right time to start establishing the right habits.

## Procrastination Does Not Pay

Healthy choices are easy to put off until some future date. But procrastination, especially concerning matters of personal health, is, at best, foolish and, at worst, dangerous. If you feel the need to improve your physical health, don't wait for New Year's Day; don't even wait until tomorrow. The time to begin living a healthier life is the moment you finish reading this sentence.

# How Many Calories?

Of a thousand American adults who were surveyed in a recent poll, eighty-eight percent were unable to accurately estimate how many calories they should consume each day to maintain their weight. Consequently, these adults didn't know how many calories they should consume if they wanted to lose weight.

Thankfully, in these days of easy Internet information, it isn't very difficult to discover how many calories you need. So do the research and find your calorie target. Then, aim for the bull's-eye that leads to better health and a longer life.

## What God Wants for You

Since God loves you, and since He wants the very best for you, don't you believe that He also wants you to enjoy a healthy lifestyle? Of course He does. And since a healthy lifestyle is what God wants for you, isn't it what you should want, too?

## More from God's Word About the Simple Life

*A simple life in the Fear-of-God is better than a rich life with a ton of headaches.*

Proverbs 15:16 MSG

*Do not love the world or the things in the world. If anyone loves the world, the love of the Father is not in him.*

1 John 2:15 NKJV

*We brought nothing into the world, so we can take nothing out. But, if we have food and clothes, we will be satisfied with that.*

1 Timothy 6:7-8 NCV

*So think clearly and exercise self-control. Look forward to the special blessings that will come to you at the return of Jesus Christ.*

1 Peter 1:13 NLT

*For the grace of God has been revealed, bringing salvation to all people. And we are instructed to turn from godless living and sinful pleasures. We should live in this evil world with self-control, right conduct, and devotion to God.*

Titus 2:11-12 NLT

# The Right Kind of Exercise for You

*He gives strength to the weary and strengthens the powerless.*
Isaiah 40:29 HCSB

If you want to attain and maintain a healthy lifestyle, it's important to engage in a consistent exercise program. Implementing a plan of regular, sensible exercise is one way of ensuring that you've done your part to care for the body that God has given you.

Dr. Kenneth Cooper observed, "Physical activity achieved at any level is an essential ingredient in slowing down the process of aging and turning life into a far more useful, enjoyable—and independent—affair." So what's the right kind of exercise for you? That's a question for you and your doctor. But whether you're running marathons or walking around the block, it's important to stay as active as you can, as long as you can.

No one can force you to exercise . . . you'll need to make that decision on your own. And if you genuinely desire to please God, it's a decision that you will make today.

## More from God's Word

*And He said to me, "My grace is sufficient for you, for My strength is made perfect in weakness."*

2 Corinthians 12:9 NKJV

*You, therefore, my child, be strong in the grace that is in Christ Jesus.*

2 Timothy 2:1 HCSB

*The Lord is my strength and my song; He has become my salvation.*

Exodus 15:2 HCSB

*But those who wait on the Lord shall renew their strength; they shall mount up with wings like eagles, they shall run and not be weary, they shall walk and not faint.*

Isaiah 40:31 NKJV

### Remember This:

Your exercise regimen should be sensible, enjoyable, safe, and consistent.

## More Thoughts About the Importance of Exercise

People who exercise at least 3 hours a week tend to eat a more balanced and a healthier diet.

Dr. Walt Larimore

Give at least two hours every day to exercise, for health must not be sacrificed to learning. A strong body makes the mind strong.

Thomas Jefferson

An early morning walk is a blessing for the whole day.

Henry David Thoreau

Fitness is a state of body and a state of mind: if your mind leads, your body will follow.

Marie T. Freeman

## Moderation Day by Day

John Maxwell observed, "The key to healthy eating is moderation and managing what you eat every day." And he was right. Crash diets don't usually work, but sensible eating habits do work, so plan your meals accordingly.

# Sensible Exercise

A healthy lifestyle includes regular, sensible physical exercise. How much exercise is right for you? That's a decision that you should make in consultation with your physician. But make no mistake: if you sincerely desire to be a thoughtful caretaker of the body that God has given you, exercise is important.

Once you begin a regular exercise program, you'll discover that the benefits to you are not only physical but also psychological. Regular exercise allows you to build your muscles while you're clearing your head and lifting your spirits.

So, if you've been taking your body for granted, today is a wonderful day to change. You can start slowly, perhaps with a brisk walk around the block. As your stamina begins to build, so too will your sense of satisfaction. And, you'll be comforted by the knowledge that you've done your part to protect and preserve the precious body that God has entrusted to your care.

**God Rewards Obedience**

God's instructions are clear: He rewards wise behaviors and He punishes misbehavior. A commitment to a sensible program is one way of being wise, and it's also one way of pleasing God every day.

# How Much Exercise?

How much exercise is right for you? That's a decision that you should make in consultation with your physician. But make no mistake: if you want to be a thoughtful caretaker of the only body you'll ever have in this world, exercise is important.

The benefits of exercise are not only physical but also psychological. Regular exercise allows you to build your muscles while you're clearing your head and lifting your spirits. So, if you're not already working out, talk to your doctor and then start an exercise regimen that's right for you. When you do, you'll be doing both your body and your mind a favor . . . and they'll both thank you for it.

**Remake Your Environment:**

If you're trying to remodel yourself, you'll need to remodel your environment, too. In order to decrease temptations and increase the probability of success, you should take a long, hard look at your home, your office, and the places you frequently visit. Then, you must do whatever you can to move yourself as far as possible from the temptations that you intend to defeat.

## More from God's Word About Your Priorities

*Don't abandon wisdom, and she will watch over you; love her, and she will guard you.*

Proverbs 4:6 HCSB


*And I pray this: that your love will keep on growing in knowledge and every kind of discernment, so that you can determine what really matters and can be pure and blameless in the day of Christ.*

Philippians 1:9 HCSB


*So teach us to number our days, that we may gain a heart of wisdom.*

Psalm 90:12 NKJV


*For where your treasure is, there your heart will be also.*

Luke 12:34 HCSB


*He said to them all, "If anyone desires to come after Me, let him deny himself, and take up his cross daily, and follow Me. For whoever desires to save his life will lose it, but whoever loses his life for My sake will save it."*

Luke 9:23-24 NKJV

## Notes to Yourself

In the space below, make notes about the spiritual, psychological, and physical benefits you experience when you exercise.

_____

_____

_____

_____

_____

_____

_____

_____

_____

_____

_____

_____

_____

## Principle 6

# In the Matter of Health, Your Choices Matter

*I have set before you life and death, blessing and curse. Choose life so that you and your descendants may live, love the Lord your God, obey Him, and remain faithful to Him. For He is your life, and He will prolong your life in the land the Lord swore to give to your fathers Abraham, Isaac, and Jacob.*

Deuteronomy 30:19-20 HCSB

E ach day, we make thousands of small choices concerning the things that we do and the things we think. Most of these choices are made without too much forethought. In fact, most of us go about our daily lives spending a significant portion simply reacting to events. Often, our actions are simply the result of impulse or habit. God asks that we slow down long enough to think about the choices that we make, and He asks that we make those choices in accordance with His commandments.

The God's Word teaches us that our bodies are "temples" that belong to Him (1 Corinthians 6:19-20). We are commanded (not encouraged, not advised, not asked, commanded!) to treat our bodies with respect and honor. We do so by making wise choices and by making those choices consistently over an extended period of time.

Do you sincerely seek to improve the overall quality of your health? Then vow to yourself and to God that you will begin making the kind of wise choices that will lead to a longer, healthier, happier life. The responsibility for those choices is yours. And so are the rewards.

## More from God's Word

*I always do my best to have a clear conscience toward God and men.*

Acts 24:16 HCSB

*The thing you should want most is God's kingdom and doing what God wants. Then all these other things you need will be given to you.*

Matthew 6:33 NCV

*If you don't know what you're doing, pray to the Father. He loves to help. You'll get his help, and won't be condescended to when you ask for it. Ask boldly, believingly, without a second thought. People who "worry their prayers" are like wind-whipped waves. Don't think you're going to get anything from the Master that way, adrift at sea, keeping all your options open.*

James 1:5-8 MSG

### Remember This:
First you make choices . . . and soon those choices begin to shape your life. That's why you must make smart choices . . . or face the consequences of making dumb ones.

*The wise people will shine
like the brightness of the sky.
Those who teach others to live right
will shine like stars forever and ever.*

—

Daniel 12:3 NCV

## More Thoughts About Making Wise Choices

Since behaviors become habits, make them work with you and not against you.

E. Stanley Jones

He who does not overcome small faults, shall fall little by little into greater ones.

Thomas à Kempis

The simple fact is that if we sow a lifestyle that is in direct disobedience to God's revealed Word, we ultimately reap disaster.

Charles Swindoll

Virtue—even attempted virtue—brings light; indulgence brings fog.

C. S. Lewis

## If Someone Else Is Cooking Your Meals . . .

If someone else is cooking your meals, ask that person to help you plan a healthier diet. Without the cooperation of the person who cooks your food, you'll have an incredibly difficult time sticking to a healthier diet.

# Eat Less, Walk More

Are you chained to a desk or trapped in a sedentary lifestyle? And are you waiting for something big to happen before you revolutionize your exercise habits? If so, wait no more. In fact, you can start today by substituting a light snack and a healthy walk for that calorie-laden lunch.

If you're in reasonably good shape, a nice healthy walk can be a great substitute for a big sit-down meal. So don't underestimate the benefits of a good walk. It's a great way to burn a few calories, to get some fresh air, and to improve your life.

### Many Chances to Make Good Decisions

Physical fitness is not the result of a single decision that is made "once and for all." Physical fitness results from thousands of decisions that are made day after day, week after week, and year after year.

# Always Keep Learning

Today is your classroom: what will you learn? Will you use today's experiences as tools for personal, spiritual, and physical improvement, or will you ignore the lessons that life and God are trying to teach you? Will you carefully study God's Word, and will you apply His teachings to the experiences of everyday life? The events of today have much to teach. You have much to learn. May you live—and learn—accordingly.

## High-Quality Choices Lead to a High-Quality Life

Every step of your life's journey is a choice . . . and the quality of those choices determines the quality of the journey.

## More from God's Word About Lifetime Learning

*A wise person pays attention to correction that will improve his life.*

Proverbs 15:31 ICB

*Remember what you are taught, and listen carefully to words of knowledge.*

Proverbs 23:12 NCV

*The fear of the Lord is the beginning of knowledge, but fools despise wisdom and discipline.*

Proverbs 1:7 NIV

*The knowledge of the secrets of the kingdom of heaven has been given to you....*

Matthew 13:11 NIV

*It is not good to have zeal without knowledge, nor to be hasty and miss the way.*

Proverbs 19:2 NIV

# Healthy Priorities

*Dear friend, I pray that you may prosper in every way and be in good health, just as your soul prospers.*
3 John 1:2 HCSB

When it comes to matters of physical, spiritual, and emotional health, Christians possess an infallible guidebook: the Holy Bible. And, when it comes to matters concerning fitness—whether physical, emotional, or spiritual—God's Word can help us establish clear priorities that can guide our steps and our lives.

It's easy to talk about establishing clear priorities for maintaining physical and spiritual health, but it's much more difficult to live according to those priorities. For busy believers living in a demanding world, placing first things first can be difficult indeed. Why? Because so many people are expecting so many things from us!

If you're having trouble prioritizing your day—or if you're having trouble sticking to a plan that enhances your spiritual and physical health—perhaps you've been trying to organize your life according to your own plans, not God's. A better strategy, of course, is to take your daily obligations and place them in the hands of the One who created you. To do so, you must prioritize your day according to God's commandments, and you must seek His will and His wisdom in all matters.

Would you like to embark upon a personal journey to better fitness? If so, you should remind yourself that on every step of that journey, you have a traveling companion: your Heavenly Father. Turn the concerns of this day over to Him—prayerfully, earnestly, and often. And trust Him to give you the strength you need to become the kind of person He wants you to become.

### Remember This:

Fitness is a journey, not a destination. Achieving physical fitness—and maintaining it—is a seven-day-a-week assignment. If you don't make physical fitness a priority, your health will suffer.

## More from God's Word

*Do you not know that your body is a sanctuary of the Holy Spirit who is in you, whom you have from God? You are not your own, for you were bought at a price; therefore glorify God in your body.*

1 Corinthians 6:19-20 HCSB

*I have come that they may have life, and that they may have it more abundantly.*

John 10:10 NKJV

*I urge you to live a life worthy of the calling you have received.*

Ephesians 4:1 NIV

*My cup runs over. Surely goodness and mercy shall follow me all the days of my life; and I will dwell in the house of the Lord forever.*

Psalm 23:5-6 NKJV

*Is any among you afflicted? Let him pray.*

James 5:13 KJV

## More Thoughts About Health

Ultimate healing and the glorification of the body are certainly among the blessings of Calvary for the believing Christian. Immediate healing is not guaranteed.

*Warren Wiersbe*

The effective Christians of history have been men and women of great personal discipline—mental discipline, discipline of the body, discipline of the tongue, and discipline of the emotion.

*Billy Graham*

Exercise: you don't have time not to.

*Anonymous*

## Become an Expert

You don't have to attend medical school to understand the basic principles of maintaining a healthy lifestyle. In fact, many of the things you need to know are contained in this text. But don't stop here. Vow to make yourself an expert on the care and feeding of the body that God has given you. In today's information-packed world, becoming an expert isn't a very hard thing to do.

# Know Your Blood Pressure

High blood pressure can cause heart attacks, strokes, and plenty of other serious health problems. The good news is that high blood pressure is usually treatable with medication, or lifestyle changes, or both. But you won't know you need treatment unless you know your blood pressure. Thankfully, blood pressure cuffs can be found just about everywhere, in many drug stores and even in some supermarkets. Or, if you prefer, you can buy your own blood pressure cuff to use at home.

So remember this: you don't have to wait for a doctor's appointment to check your blood pressure. You can monitor your own blood pressure in between visits to the doctor's office, and that's precisely what you should do.

### Don't Trust the Media's Messages

Many of the messages that you receive from the media are specifically designed to sell you products that interfere with your spiritual, physical, or emotional health. God takes great interest in your health; the moguls from Madison Avenue take great interest in your pocketbook. Trust God.

# The Gift of Life

Life is a glorious gift from God. Treat it that way.

This day, like every other, is filled to the brim with opportunities, challenges, and choices. But, no choice that you make is more important than the choice you make concerning God. Today, you will either place Him at the center of your life—or not—and the consequences of that choice have implications that are both temporal and eternal.

Sometimes, we don't intentionally neglect God; we simply allow ourselves to become overwhelmed with the demands of everyday life. And then, without our even realizing it, we gradually drift away from the One we need most. Thankfully, God never drifts away from us. He remains always present, always steadfast, always loving.

As you begin this day, place God and His Son where they belong: in your head, in your prayers, on your lips, and in your heart. And then, with God as your guide and companion, let the journey begin . . .

### Make Exercise Fun

Make exercise enjoyable. Your workouts should be a source of pleasure and satisfaction, not a form of self-imposed punishment. Find a way to exercise your body that is satisfying, effective, and fun.

## More from God's Word About Life

*I urge you now to live the life to which God called you.*

Ephesians 4:1 NKJV

*Shout triumphantly to the Lord, all the earth. Serve the Lord with gladness; come before Him with joyful songs.*

Psalm 100:1-2 HCSB

*Rejoice in the Lord always. Again I will say, rejoice!*

Philippians 4:4 NKJV

*Jesus told him, "I am the way, the truth, and the life. No one comes to the Father except through Me."*

John 14:6 HCSB

*He who follows righteousness and mercy finds life, righteousness and honor.*

Proverbs 21:21 NKJV

## Notes to Yourself

In the space below, write down ways that you can be more proactive about your health.

_____

_____

_____

_____

_____

_____

_____

_____

_____

_____

_____

_____

# Principle 7

# God Wants You to Learn How to Discipline Yourself

*I am able to do all things through Him who strengthens me.*
Philippians 4:13 HCSB

Physical fitness requires discipline: the discipline to exercise regularly and the discipline to eat sensibly—it's as simple as that. But here's the catch: understanding the need for discipline is easy, but leading a disciplined life can be hard for most of us. Why? Because it's usually more fun to eat a second piece of cake than it is to jog a second lap around the track. But, as we survey the second helpings that all too often find their way on to our plates, we should consider this: as Christians, we are instructed to lead disciplined lives, and when we behave in undisciplined ways, we are living outside God's will.

God's Word reminds us again and again that our Creator expects us to be disciplined in our thoughts and disciplined in our actions. God doesn't reward laziness, misbehavior, apathy, or shortsightedness. To the contrary, He expects believers to behave with dignity and self-control.

We live in a world in which leisure is glorified and consumption is commercialized. But God has other plans. He did not create us for lives of gluttony of sloth; He created us for far greater things.

Life's greatest rewards seldom fall into our laps; to the contrary, our greatest accomplishments usually require lots of work, which is perfectly fine with God. After all, He knows that we're up to the task, and He has big plans for us; may we, as disciplined believers, always be worthy of those plans.

## More from God's Word

*No discipline seems enjoyable at the time, but painful. Later on, however, it yields the fruit of peace and righteousness to those who have been trained by it.*

Hebrews 12:11 HCSB

*For this very reason, make every effort to supplement your faith with goodness, goodness with knowledge, knowledge with self-control, self-control with endurance, endurance with godliness.*

2 Peter 1:5-6 HCSB

*I discipline my body and bring it under strict control, so that after preaching to others, I myself will not be disqualified.*

1 Corinthians 9:27 HCSB

### Remember This:

Discipline matters. It takes discipline to strengthen your faith; it takes discipline to improve your fitness.

Work is doing it.
Discipline is doing it every day.
Diligence is doing it well every day.

—

Dave Ramsey

## More Thoughts About Discipline

If one examines the secret behind a championship football team, a magnificent orchestra, or a successful business, the principal ingredient is invariably discipline.

*James Dobson*

Discipline is training that develops and corrects.

*Charles Stanley*

God cannot build character without our cooperation. If we resist Him, then He chastens us into submission. But, if we submit to Him, then He can accomplish His work. He is not satisfied with a halfway job. God wants a perfect work; He wants a finished product that is mature and complete.

*Warren Wiersbe*

The Bible calls for discipline.

*Billy Graham*

## Discipline Is Not a Four-letter Word

Exercising discipline should never be viewed as an imposition or as a form of punishment; far from it. Discipline is the means by which you can take control of your life (which, by the way, is far better than letting your life control you).

# The Source of Strength

Where do you go to find strength? The gym? The health food store? The espresso bar? There's a better source of strength, of course, and that source is God. He is a never-ending source of strength and courage if you call upon Him.

Are you an energized Christian? You should be. But if you're not, you must seek strength and renewal from the source that will never fail: that source, of course, is your Heavenly Father. And rest assured—when you sincerely petition Him, He will give you all the strength you need to live victoriously for Him.

Have you "tapped in" to the power of God? Have you turned your life and your heart over to Him, or are you muddling along under your own power? The answer to this question will determine the quality of your life here on earth and the destiny of your life throughout all eternity. So start tapping in—and remember that when it comes to strength, God is the Ultimate Source.

### Start Now

If you're genuinely planning on becoming a disciplined person "some day" in the distant future, you're deluding yourself. The best day to begin exercising self-discipline is this one.

# Small Steps

I f you want to become more physically fit, you don't have to make one giant leap. You can start with many small steps, and you should. When it comes to any new exercise regimen, starting slowly and improving gradually is the smart way to do it.

Crash diets usually crash. And fitness fads fade. But sensible exercise, when combined with a moderate diet, produces results that last.

So if you're determined to improve the state of your health, remember that consistency is the key. Start slowly, avoid injury, be consistent, and expect gradual improvement, not instant success.

### The Book of Proverbs Has Much to Teach

If you're looking for words of wisdom that extol the virtues of a disciplined lifestyle, the Book of Proverbs is a wonderful place to start. It has 31 chapters, one for each day of the month. If you read Proverbs regularly, and if you take its teachings to heart, you'll become a more disciplined person. And God will smile.

## More from God's Word About God's Strength

*Be of good courage, and let us be strong for our people and for the cities of our God. And may the Lord do what is good in His sight.*

1 Chronicles 19:13 NKJV

*Do you not know? Have you not heard? The Everlasting God, the LORD, the Creator of the ends of the earth does not become weary or tired. His understanding is inscrutable. He gives strength to the weary, and to him who lacks might He increases power. Though youths grow weary and tired, and vigorous young men stumble badly, yet those who wait for the LORD will gain new strength; they will mount up with wings like eagles, they will run and not get tired, they will walk and not become weary.*

Isaiah 40:28–31 NASB

*He said unto me, My grace is sufficient for thee: for my strength is made perfect in weakness.*

2 Corinthians 12:9 KJV

*The LORD is my strength and my song . . . .*

Exodus 15:2 NIV

*The LORD is a refuge for His people
and a stronghold.*

—

Joel 3:16 NASB

# Your Body, Your Choices

*So then each of us shall give account of himself to God.*
Romans 14:12 NKJV

As adults, each of us bears a personal responsibility for the general state of our own physical health. Certainly, various aspects of health are beyond our control: illness sometimes strikes even the healthiest men and women. But for most of us, physical health is a choice: it is the result of hundreds of small decisions that we make every day of our lives. If we make decisions that promote good health, our bodies respond. But if we fall into bad habits and undisciplined lifestyles, we suffer tragic consequences.

Do you sincerely desire to improve your physical fitness? If so, start by taking personal responsibility for the body that God has given you. Then, make the solemn pledge to yourself that you will begin to make the changes that are required to enjoy a longer, healthier, happier life.

**Remember This:**
You're the human being whom God has entrusted with the responsibility of caring for your body. So it's always the right time to become proactive about your health.

*So teach us to number our days,
that we may gain a heart of wisdom.*

—

Psalm 90:12 NKJV

## More from God's Word

*Even a young man is known by his actions—by whether his behavior is pure and upright.*

Proverbs 20:11 HCSB

*But each person should examine his own work, and then he will have a reason for boasting in himself alone, and not in respect to someone else. For each person will have to carry his own load.*

Galatians 6:4-5 HCSB

*You will show me the path of life; in Your presence is fullness of joy; at Your right hand are pleasures forevermore.*

Psalm 16:11 NKJV

*Light shines on the godly, and joy on those who do right. May all who are godly be happy in the Lord and praise his holy name.*

Psalm 97:11-12 NLT

## More Thoughts About Taking Responsibility

If you don't take care of your body, how can you expect your body to take care of you?

*Marie T. Freeman*

As we make an offering of our work, we find the truth of a principle Jesus taught: Fulfillment is not a goal to achieve, but always the by-product of a sacrifice.

*Elisabeth Elliot*

Whether we know it or not, whether we agree with it or not, whether we practice it or not, whether we like it or not, we are accountable to one another.

*Charles Stanley*

## Accept Responsibility

It's easy to blame other people for the current state of your health. You live in a world where it's fashionable to blame food manufacturers, doctors, and fast food restaurants, to mention but a few. Yet none of these folks force food into your mouth, and they don't force you to sit on the sofa when you should be exercising! So remember: it's your body . . . and it's your responsibility.

# The Futility of Blame

When our unhealthy habits lead to poor health, we find it all too easy to look beyond ourselves and assign blame. In fact, we live in a society where blame has become a national obsession: we blame cigarette manufacturers, restaurants, and food producers, to name only a few. But to blame others is to miss the point: we, and we alone, are responsible for the way that we treat our bodies. And the sooner that we accept that responsibility, the sooner we can assert control over our bodies and our lives.

So, when it comes to your own body, assume control and accept responsibility. It's a great way to live and a great way to stay healthy.

### Good Intentions Are Not Enough

The road to poor health is paved with good intentions. Until you make exercise a high priority in your life, your good intentions will soon give way to old habits. So give your exercise regimen a position of high standing on your daily to-do list.

# Action springs not from thought, but from a readiness for responsibility.

—

Dietrich Bonhoeffer

# Beware the Checkout Line

Unless you're a hermit living on a deserted island, you pass through those check-out lines awash in tabloids and tasty treats. Of course, the retailers' strategy is straightforward: to get you to make a quick impulse purchase. So most times, you'll come face-to-face with an assortment of candies, chips, and pre-packed cookies. What's needed by you is willpower. Otherwise, you'll form the habit of impulsively munching on fat-laden, life-shortening snacks.

So here's your rule for the checkout lines of life: yield not to temptation. Keep your eyes and your hands to yourself, and leave all those unhealthy snacks on the shelf . . . or else.

**Building a Better Self-Image**

When you accept responsibilities and fulfill them, you'll feel better about yourself. When you avoid your obligations, you won't. Act accordingly.

## More from God's Word About Doing the Right Thing

*The righteous one will live by his faith.*

Habakkuk 2:4 HCSB

*And the world is passing away, and the lust of it; but he who does the will of God abides forever.*

1 John 2:17 NKJV

*Because the eyes of the Lord are on the righteous and His ears are open to their request. But the face of the Lord is against those who do evil.*

1 Peter 3:12 HCSB

*Flee from youthful passions, and pursue righteousness, faith, love, and peace, along with those who call on the Lord from a pure heart.*

2 Timothy 2:22 HCSB

*Sow righteousness for yourselves and reap faithful love; break up your untilled ground. It is time to seek the Lord until He comes and sends righteousness on you like the rain.*

Hosea 10:12 HCSB

## Notes to Yourself

In the space below, write down the benefits that will be yours when you take personal responsibility for your exercise and your diet.

_____

_____

_____

_____

_____

_____

_____

_____

_____

_____

_____

_____

_____

# God Can Energize Your Life and Restore Your Health

*But those who trust in the Lord will renew their strength;*
*they will soar on wings like eagles; they will run and*
*not grow weary; they will walk and not faint.*
Isaiah 40:31 HCSB

As you make the journey toward improved fitness, you'll undoubtedly run out of energy from time to time. When it happens, you can turn to God for strength and for guidance.

Andrew Murray observed, "Where there is much prayer, there will be much of the Spirit; where there is much of the Spirit, there will be ever-increasing power." These words remind us that the ultimate source of our strength is God. When we turn to Him—for guidance, for enlightenment, and for strength—we will not be disappointed.

Are you feeling exhausted? Are your emotions on edge? If so, it's time to turn things over to God in prayer. Are you weak or worried? Take the time—or, more accurately, make the time—to delve deeply into God's Holy Word. Are you spiritually depleted? Call upon fellow believers to support you, and call upon Christ to renew your spirit and your life. When you do, you'll discover that the Creator of the universe has the power to make all things new . . . including you.

### Remember This:

For the journey through life, you need energy. The best source of energy, of course, is God. So if you're wise, you'll ask the Creator to energize you and guide you today and every day.

## More from God's Word

*But Jesus looked at them and said, "With men this is impossible, but with God all things are possible."*

Matthew 19:26 HCSB

*You are the God who works wonders; You revealed Your strength among the peoples.*

Psalm 77:14 HCSB

*Proclaim the power of God, whose majesty is over Israel, whose power is in the skies. You are awesome, O God, in your sanctuary; the God of Israel gives power and strength to his people. Praise be to God!*

Psalm 68:34-35 NIV

*Do not lack diligence; be fervent in spirit; serve the Lord.*

Romans 12:11 HCSB

*Whatever work you do, do your best, because you are going to the grave, where there is no working . . . .*

Ecclesiastes 9:10 NCV

## More Thoughts About Renewal

Jesus taught us by example to get out of the rat race and recharge our batteries.

*Barbara Johnson*

Troubles we bear trustfully can bring us a fresh vision of God and a new outlook on life, an outlook of peace and hope.

*Billy Graham*

Hope can give us life. It can provide energy that would otherwise do us in completely if we tried to operate in our own strength.

*Barbara Johnson*

To win one's joy through struggle is better than to yield to melancholy.

*André Gide*

## Finding the Energy to Do God's Work

It takes energy to do God's work. And a well-rested Christian can be a much more effective worker for God. So plan your life, and your sleep, accordingly.

# Beware of Restaurant Fare

In the good old days, dining out used to be an occasional treat for most families. Now, it's more of an everyday occurrence. But there's a catch: most restaurants aim for taste first, price second, and health a distant third. But you should think health first. So the next time you head out for a burger, a bagel, or any other fast food, take a minute to read the fine print that's usually posted on the wall. You may find out that the healthy-sounding treat is actually a calorie-bomb in disguise.

## More Exercise Equals Less Stress

As exercise increases, stress usually decreases. So, if you want less stress in your life, you should exercise more frequently.

# Your Energy and God's Promises

A ll of us have moments when we feel exhausted. All of us suffer through tough times, difficult days, and perplexing periods of our lives. Thankfully, God promises to give us comfort and strength if we turn to Him.

If you're a person with too many demands and too few hours in which to meet them, it's probably time to examine your priorities while you pare down your daily to-do list. While you're at it, take time to focus upon God and His love for you. Then, ask Him for the wisdom to prioritize your life and the strength to fulfill your responsibilities. God will give you the energy to do the most important things on today's to-do list if you ask Him. So ask Him . . . today.

## Energy Directly from the Source

Feeling exhausted? Try this: Start getting more sleep each night; begin a program of regular, sensible exercise; avoid harmful food and drink; and turn your problems over to God. And, the greatest of these is "turn your problems over to God."

## More from God's Word About Bible Study

*All Scripture is inspired by God and is profitable for teaching, for rebuking, for correcting, for training in righteousness, so that the man of God may be complete, equipped for every good work.*

2 Timothy 3:16-17 HCSB

*Man shall not live by bread alone, but by every word that proceeds from the mouth of God.*

Matthew 4:4 NKJV

*Heaven and earth will pass away, but My words will never pass away.*

Matthew 24:35 HCSB

*For the word of God is living and effective and sharper than any two-edged sword, penetrating as far as to divide soul, spirit, joints, and marrow; it is a judge of the ideas and thoughts of the heart.*

Hebrews 4:12 HCSB

*For I am not ashamed of the gospel, because it is God's power for salvation to everyone who believes.*

Romans 1:16 HCSB

# Getting Enough Rest?

*Come to Me, all you who are weary and burdened,*
*and I will give you rest.*
Matthew 11:28-30 NKJV

Even the most inspired Christians can, from time to time, find themselves running on empty. The demands of daily life can drain us of our strength and rob us of the joy that is rightfully ours in Christ. When we find ourselves tired, discouraged, or worse, there is a source from which we can draw the power needed to recharge our spiritual batteries. That source is God.

God intends that His children lead joyous lives filled with abundance and peace. But sometimes, abundance and peace seem very far away. It is then that we must turn to God for renewal, and when we do, He will restore us.

God expects us to work hard, but He also intends for us to rest. When we fail to take the rest that we need, we do a disservice to ourselves and to our families.

Is your spiritual battery running low? Is your energy on the wane? Are your emotions frayed? If so, it's time to turn your thoughts and your prayers to God. And when you're finished, it's time to rest.

## More from God's Word

*I said to myself, "Relax and rest. God has showered you with blessings."*

Psalm 116:7 MSG

*And be not conformed to this world: but be ye transformed by the renewing of your mind.*

Romans 12:2 KJV

*And the apostles gathered themselves together unto Jesus, and told him all things, both what they had done, and what they had taught. And he said unto them, Come ye yourselves apart into a desert place, and rest a while.*

Mark 6:30-31 HCSB

*I will lift up mine eyes unto the hills, from whence cometh my help. My help cometh from the Lord, which made heaven and earth.*

Psalm 121:1-2 KJV

### Remember This:

God wants you to get enough rest. The world wants you to burn the candle at both ends. Trust God.

## More Thoughts About Getting Enough Rest

Satan does some of his worst work on exhausted Christians when nerves are frayed and their minds are faint.

Vance Havner

One reason so much American Christianity is a mile wide and an inch deep is that Christians are simply tired. Sometimes you need to kick back and rest for Jesus' sake.

Dennis Swanberg

Take a rest; a field that has rested gives a bountiful crop.

Ovid

Early to bed and early to rise, makes a man healthy, wealthy, and wise.

Ben Franklin

## Getting 8 Hours Is Important

Most adults need about eight hours of sleep each night. If you're depriving yourself of much needed sleep in order to stay up and watch late night television, you've developed a bad habit. Instead, do yourself a favor: turn off the TV and go to bed.

# If You're Having Trouble Sleeping, Consider the Following Tips

1.  Reduce your intake of caffeine or eliminate caffeine entirely from your diet. The residual effects of too much coffee (or too many caffeine-loaded soft drinks) may be contributing to your sleeplessness.

2.  At least one hour before bedtime, begin the process of preparing for sleep by putting yourself into a calmer state. Don't watch television programs that might upset you or "get your juices flowing." Instead, engage in quieter pursuits (such as reading) in order to ready yourself for a good night's sleep.

3.  If you can't fall asleep quickly, don't lay in bed and worry about the fact that you are not sleeping. Get up, pick up a book, and read until you feel tired. Then go back to bed. Your bed should be a place for sleeping, not a place for worrying.

4.  Establish regular sleep patterns by getting up at the same time every day. Even if you don't fall asleep until a very late hour, force yourself out of bed at the same time each morning. This practice will, within a few weeks, help you establish a more normal pattern of sleep.

5. Troubles and worries are always magnified during the nighttime hours. If you are too worried about a particular topic to fall asleep, do not lay in bed and obsess over the problem. Instead, get up, take pencil and paper, and write down your worries, along with an action plan to solve them.

6. Engage in sensible physical exercise on a regular basis.

7. If you or someone close to you feels that your lack of sleep is posing a hazard to your physical or emotional well-being, consult your physician.

8. Remember the words of Victor Hugo: "Have courage for all the great sorrows of life and patience for the small ones. And when you have finished your daily task, go to sleep. God is awake."

### Make It Fun

If you genuinely want to exercise more, find exercise that you enjoy. And if you can't seem to find exercise that you enjoy, search for ways to make your current exercise program a little less painful and a little more fun.

Come, come, come unto Me,
Weary and sore distressed;
Come, come, come unto Me,
Come unto Me and rest.

—

Fanny Crosby

# Exhausted?
# Try Turning Off the TV
# a Little Earlier

You live in a world that tempts you to stay up late—very late. But too much late-night TV, combined with too little sleep, is a prescription for exhaustion, ill health, ill temper, or all three. So do yourself, your boss, and your loved ones a big favor. Arrange your TV schedule and your life so you get eight hours of sleep every night.

Since you can't cheat Mr. Sandman, don't even try. When in doubt, do the smart thing: do whatever it takes to get the sleep you need. It's the smart way to schedule your day and your life.

### Angry? Maybe You're Just Tired

Oftentimes, our anger is nothing more than exhaustion in disguise. When in doubt, get eight hours sleep.

## More from God's Word About Peace

*And the peace of God, which surpasses every thought, will guard your hearts and your minds in Christ Jesus. Finally brothers, whatever is true, whatever is honorable, whatever is just, whatever is pure, whatever is lovely, whatever is commendable—if there is any moral excellence and if there is any praise—dwell on these things.*

Philippians 4:7-8 HCSB

*Abundant peace belongs to those who love Your instruction; nothing makes them stumble.*

Psalm 119:165 HCSB

*And let the peace of God rule in your hearts...and be ye thankful.*

Colossians 3:15 KJV

*You will keep in perfect peace him whose mind is steadfast, because he trusts in you.*

Isaiah 26:3 NIV

*I have told you these things so that in Me you may have peace. In the world you have suffering. But take courage! I have conquered the world.*

John 16:33 HCSB

**Notes to Yourself**

In the space below, write down several things you can do
to insure that you get enough rest each night.

_____

_____

_____

_____

_____

_____

_____

_____

_____

_____

_____

_____

# Fitness Is a Form of Worship

*Worship the Lord your God and . . . serve Him only.*
Matthew 4:10 HCSB

What does worship have to do with fitness? That depends on how you define worship. If you consider worship to be a "Sunday-only" activity, an activity that occurs only inside the four walls of your local church, then fitness and worship may seem totally unrelated. But, if you view worship as an activity that impacts every facet of your life—if you consider worship to be something far more than a "one-day-a-week" obligation—then you understand that every aspect of your life is a form of worship. And that includes keeping your body physically fit.

Make no mistake: All of mankind (including you) is engaged in worship...of one kind or another. The question is not whether we worship, but what we worship. Some of us choose to worship our Heavenly Father. The result is a plentiful harvest of joy, peace, and abundance. Others distance themselves from God by placing the desire for personal gratification above the need for spiritual gratification. To do so can be a terrible mistake with eternal consequences.

Every day provides opportunities to put God where He belongs: at the center of our lives. When we do so, we worship not just with our words, but also with our deeds. And one way that we can honor our Heavenly Father is by treating our bodies with care and respect.

The Bible makes it clear: "Your body is the temple of the Holy Spirit" (1 Corinthians 6:19 NLT). Treat it that way. And consider your fitness regimen to be one way—a very important way—of worshipping God.

**Remember This:**
When you worship God with a sincere heart, He will guide your steps and bless your life.

## More from God's Word

*Worship the Lord with gladness. Come before him, singing with joy. Acknowledge that the Lord is God! He made us, and we are his. We are his people, the sheep of his pasture.*

Psalm 100:2-3 NLT

*But an hour is coming, and is now here, when the true worshipers will worship the Father in spirit and truth. Yes, the Father wants such people to worship Him. God is Spirit, and those who worship Him must worship in spirit and truth.*

John 4:23-24 HCSB

*So that at the name of Jesus every knee should bow—of those who are in heaven and on earth and under the earth—and every tongue should confess that Jesus Christ is Lord, to the glory of God the Father.*

Philippians 2:10-11 HCSB

*I rejoiced with those who said to me, "Let us go to the house of the Lord."*

Psalm 122:1 HCSB

## More Thoughts About Worship

It's the definition of worship: A hungry heart finding the Father's feast. A searching soul finding the Father's face. A wandering pilgrim spotting the Father's house. Finding God. Finding God seeking us. This is worship. This is a worshiper.

Max Lucado

Spiritual worship is focusing all we are on all He is.

Beth Moore

God asks that we worship Him with our concentrated minds as well as with our wills and emotions. A divided and scattered mind is not effective.

Catherine Marshall

Worship is your spirit responding to God's Spirit.

Rick Warren

## Don't Focus on Food; Focus on God

Don't worship food. Honor the body that God gave you by eating sensible portions of sensible foods.

# Remember the Sabbath

When God gave Moses the Ten Commandments, it became perfectly clear that our Heavenly Father intends for us to make the Sabbath a holy day, a day for worship, for contemplation, for fellowship, and for rest. Yet we live in a seven-day-a-week world, a world that all too often treats Sunday as a regular workday.

One way to strengthen your faith is by giving God at least one day each week. If you carve out the time for a day of worship and praise, you'll be amazed at the impact it will have on the rest of your week. But if you fail to honor God's day, if you treat the Sabbath as a day to work or a day to party, you'll miss out on a harvest of blessings that is only available one day each week.

How does your family observe the Lord's day? When church is over, do you treat Sunday like any other day of the week? If so, it's time to think long and hard about your family's schedule and your family's priorities. And if you've been treating Sunday as just another day, it's time to break that habit. When Sunday rolls around, don't try to fill every spare moment. Take time to rest . . . Father's orders!

## Consider Your Healthy Lifestyle a Form of Worship

When God described your body as a temple, He wasn't kidding. Show your respect for God's Word by keeping your temple in tip-top shape.

*So that at the name of Jesus every knee should bow—of those who are in heaven and on earth and under the earth—and every tongue should confess that Jesus Christ is Lord, to the glory of God the Father.*

—

Philippians 2:10-11 HCSB

# Praise Him

When is the best time to praise God? In church? Before dinner is served? When we tuck little children into bed? None of the above. The best time to praise God is all day, every day, to the greatest extent we can, with thanksgiving in our hearts.

Too many of us, even well-intentioned believers, tend to "compartmentalize" our waking hours into a few familiar categories: work, rest, play, family time, and worship. To do so is a mistake. Worship and praise should be woven into the fabric of everything we do; it should never be relegated to a weekly three-hour visit to church on Sunday morning.

Mrs. Charles E. Cowman, the author of the classic devotional text *Streams in the Desert*, wrote, "Two wings are necessary to lift our souls toward God: prayer and praise. Prayer asks. Praise accepts the answer." Today, find a little more time to lift your concerns to God in prayer, and praise Him for all that He has done. He's listening . . . and He wants to hear from you.

### Not Just Sunday Morning

Worship is not meant to be boxed up in a church building on Sunday morning. To the contrary, praise and worship should be woven into the very fabric of our lives.

## More from God's Word About Praise and Thanksgiving

*It is good to give thanks to the Lord, and to sing praises to Your name, O Most High.*

Psalm 92:1 NKJV

*And let the peace of the Messiah, to which you were also called in one body, control your hearts. Be thankful.*

Colossians 3:15 HCSB

*Therefore as you have received Christ Jesus the Lord, walk in Him, rooted and built up in Him and established in the faith, just as you were taught, and overflowing with thankfulness.*

Colossians 2:6-7 HCSB

*In everything give thanks; for this is the will of God in Christ Jesus for you.*

1 Thessalonians 5:18 NKJV

**Notes to Yourself**

In the space below, make notes about specific ways that you can worship God seven days a week.

_____

_____

_____

_____

_____

_____

_____

_____

_____

_____

_____

_____

# Addiction Equals Disaster

*Let us walk with decency, as in the daylight:*
*not in carousing and drunkenness.*
Romans 13:13 HCSB

The dictionary defines addiction as "the compulsive need for a habit-forming substance; the condition of being habitually and compulsively occupied with something." That definition is accurate, but incomplete. For Christians, addiction has an additional meaning: it means compulsively worshipping something other than God.

Ours is a highly addictive society. Why? The answer is straightforward: supply and demand. The supply of addictive substances continues to grow; the affordability and availability of these substances makes them highly attractive to consumers; and the overall demand for addictive substances has increased as more and more users have become addicted to an ever-expanding array of substances and compulsions.

You know people who are full-blown addicts—probably lots of people. If you, or someone you love, is suffering from the blight of addiction, the following ideas are worth remembering:

1. For the addict, addiction comes first. In the life of an addict, addiction rules. God, of course, commands otherwise. God says, "You shall have no other gods before Me," and He means precisely what He say (Exodus 20:3 NKJV). Our task, as believers, is to put God in His proper place: first place.

2. You cannot cure another person's addiction, but you can encourage that person to seek help. Addicts are cured when they decide, not when you decide. What you can

do is this: you can be supportive, and you can encourage the addict to find the help that he or she needs. (Luke 10:25-37)

3. If you are living with an addicted person, think about safety: yours and your family's. Addiction is life-threatening and life-shortening. Don't let someone else's addiction threaten your safety or the safety of your loved ones. (Proverbs 22:3)

4. Don't assist in prolonging the addiction: When you interfere with the negative consequences that might otherwise accompany an addict's negative behaviors, you are inadvertently "enabling" the addict to continue the destructive cycle of addiction. So don't be an enabler. (Proverbs 15:31)

5. Help is available: Lots of people have experienced addiction and lived to tell about it. They want to help. Let them. (Proverbs 27:17)

6. Cure is possible. With God's help, no addiction is incurable. And with God, no situation is hopeless. (Matthew 19:26)

**Remember This:**
You must guard your heart against addiction . . . or else.

## More from God's Word

*Don't associate with those who drink too much wine, or with those who gorge themselves on meat. For the drunkard and the glutton will become poor, and grogginess will clothe [them] in rags.*

Proverbs 23:20-21 HCSB

*And don't get drunk with wine, which leads to reckless actions, but be filled with the Spirit.*

Ephesians 5:18 HCSB

*Watch out! Don't let me find you living in careless ease and drunkenness, and filled with the worries of this life. Don't let that day catch you unaware.*

Luke 21:34 NLT

*Be sober! Be on the alert! Your adversary the Devil is prowling around like a roaring lion, looking for anyone he can devour.*

1 Peter 5:8 HCSB

*You shall have no other gods before Me.*

Exodus 20:3 NKJV

## More Thoughts About Temptation

Every moment of resistance to temptation is a victory.

Frederick William Faber

The chains of habit are too weak to be felt until they are too strong to be broken.

Samuel Johnson

If you want to form a new habit, get to work. If you want to break a bad habit, get on your knees.

Marie T. Freeman

A man may not be responsible for his last drink, but he certainly was for the first.

Billy Graham

## Relapse? Probably.

If you're on a new health regimen, you may relapse back into your old, unhealthy habits. If so, don't waste time or energy beating yourself up. If you've "fallen off the wagon," simply pick yourself up, dust yourself off, and get back on it. God was with you when you were riding that wagon the first time, He was with you when you fell, and He'll welcome you back on the wagon when you're wise enough to climb back on.

Just as iron, even without willing it,
is drawn by a magnet,
so is a slave to bad habits dragged
about by them.

—

John Climacus

# Safety Matters

We live in a world that can be a dangerous place, especially for those who are inclined toward risky behaviors. Some risk takers are easy to spot: they jump out of little airplanes, scurry up tall mountains, or race very fast automobiles.

Most risk takers, however, are not so bold; instead, they take more subtle risks that endanger themselves, their friends, and their families. They drink and drive, or they smoke cigarettes, or they neglect to fasten their seat belts, or they engage in countless other behaviors that, while not as glamorous as mountain climbing, are equally as dangerous.

This world holds enough hazards of its own without our adding to those risks by foolishly neglecting our own personal safety and the safety of those around us. So, the next time you're tempted to do something foolish, remember that the body you're putting at risk belongs not only to you, but also to God. And He hopes that you'll behave wisely.

## Addiction Destroys

You must guard your heart against dangerous temptations and life-sapping addictions . . . or else.

# You're Responsible

Remember that ultimately you and you alone are responsible for controlling your appetites. Others may warn you, help you, or encourage you, but in the end, the habits that rule your life are the very same habits that you yourself have formed. Thankfully, since you formed these habits, you can also break them—if you decide to do so.

## Sometimes, You Can't Do It Alone

If you can't seem to get a handle on your appetites, the time to address your problem is today, not tomorrow. Gather your courage and pay a visit to your pastor, to a counselor, or to a local 12-step group. Help is waiting, but you'll need to ask for it. So ask.

## More from God's Word About God's Grace

*But God, who is abundant in mercy, because of His great love that He had for us, made us alive with the Messiah even though we were dead in trespasses. By grace you are saved!*

Ephesians 2:4-5 HCSB

*My grace is sufficient for you, for My strength is made perfect in weakness.*

2 Corinthians 12:9 NKJV

*And we have seen and testify that the Father has sent the Son as Savior of the world.*

1 John 4:14 NKJV

*For by grace you are saved through faith, and this is not from yourselves; it is God's gift—not from works, so that no one can boast.*

Ephesians 2:8-9 HCSB

*In Him we have redemption through His blood, the forgiveness of our trespasses, according to the riches of His grace that He lavished on us with all wisdom and understanding.*

Ephesians 1:7-8 HCSB

## Notes to Yourself

In the space below, make a short list of the unhealthy foods or drinks that are most tempting to you. Then, ask God to help you avoid them today.

_____

_____

_____

_____

_____

_____

_____

_____

_____

_____

_____

_____

# God Wants You to Enjoy Spiritual Health

*But the fruit of the Spirit is love, joy, peace, long-suffering,*
*gentleness, goodness, faith, meekness, temperance . . . .*
Galatians 5:22-23 KJV

Are you as "spiritually fit" as you're ever going to be? Hopefully not! When it comes to your faith (and, by the way, when it comes to your fitness), God isn't done with you yet.

The journey toward spiritual maturity lasts a lifetime: As Christians, we can and should continue to grow in the love and the knowledge of our Savior as long as we live. But, if we cease to grow, either emotionally or spiritually, we do ourselves and our families a profound disservice.

If we study God's Word, if we obey His commandments, and if we live in the center of His will, we will not be "stagnant" believers; we will, instead, be growing Christians . . . and that's exactly what God wants for our lives.

In those quiet moments when we open our hearts to God, the Creator who made us keeps remaking us. He gives us direction, perspective, wisdom, and courage. He encourages us to become more fit in a variety of ways: more spiritually fit, more physically fit, and more emotionally fit.

God is willing to do His part to ensure that you remain fit. Are you willing to do yours?

**Remember This:**

Wherever you are in your spiritual journey, it's always the right time to take another step toward God.

## More from God's Word

*For this reason also, since the day we heard this, we haven't stopped praying for you. We are asking that you may be filled with the knowledge of His will in all wisdom and spiritual understanding.*

Colossians 1:9 HCSB

*I want their hearts to be encouraged and joined together in love, so that they may have all the riches of assured understanding, and have the knowledge of God's mystery—Christ.*

Colossians 2:2 HCSB

*Therefore, leaving the elementary message about the Messiah, let us go on to maturity.*

Hebrews 6:1 HCSB

*For You, O God, have tested us; You have refined us as silver is refined. You brought us into the net; You laid affliction on our backs. You have caused men to ride over our heads; we went through fire and through water; but You brought us out to rich fulfillment.*

Psalm 66:10–12 NKJV

*But grow in the grace and knowledge of our Lord and Savior Jesus Christ. To Him be the glory both now and to the day of eternity.*

2 Peter 3:18 HCSB

## More Thoughts About Spiritual Growth

Spiritual growth consists most in the growth of the root, which is out of sight.

Matthew Henry

A Christian is never in a state of completion but always in the process of becoming.

Martin Luther

We set our eyes on the finish line, forgetting the past, and straining toward the mark of spiritual maturity and fruitfulness.

Vonette Bright

You are either becoming more like Christ every day or you're becoming less like Him. There is no neutral position in the Lord.

Stormie Omartian

## It Takes Time

Spiritual growth is not instantaneous . . . and neither, for that matter, is the attainment of a physically fit body. So be patient. You should expect a few ups and downs along the way, but you should also expect to see progress over time.

# Perfection? Forget About It

As you begin to work toward improved physical and emotional health, don't expect perfection. Of course you should work hard; of course you should be disciplined; of course you should do your best. But then, when you've given it your best effort, you should be accepting of yourself, imperfect though you may be.

In heaven, we will know perfection. Here on earth, we have a few short years to wrestle with the challenges of imperfection. Let us accept these lives that God has given us—and these bodies which are ours for a brief time here on earth—with open, loving arms.

### Obedience to God Is Essential

It's simple: When you're treating your body like a temple, you're obeying God; when you're abusing your body, you're disobeying Him.

# Always Growing in Your Faith

When it comes to your faith, God doesn't intend for you to stand still. He wants you to keep moving and growing. In fact, God's plan for you includes a lifetime of prayer, praise, and spiritual growth.

As a Christian, you should continue to grow in the love and the knowledge of your Savior as long as you live. How? By studying God's Word every day, by obeying His commandments, and by allowing His Son to reign over your heart, that's how.

Are you continually seeking to become a more mature believer? Hopefully so, because that's exactly what you owe to yourself and to God . . . but not necessarily in that order.

### Spiritual Growth Is Always Possible

How do you know if you can still keep growing as a Christian? Check your pulse. If it's still beating, then you can still keep growing.

## More from God's Word About Trusting God

*Lord, I turn my hope to You. My God, I trust in You. Do not let me be disgraced; do not let my enemies gloat over me.*

Psalm 25:1-2 HCSB

*He granted their request because they trusted in Him.*

1 Chronicles 5:20 HCSB

*The one who understands a matter finds success, and the one who trusts in the Lord will be happy.*

Proverbs 16:20 HCSB

*The fear of man is a snare, but the one who trusts in the Lord is protected.*

Proverbs 29:25 HCSB

*Those who trust in the Lord are like Mount Zion. It cannot be shaken; it remains forever.*

Psalm 125:1 HCSB

# Protecting Your Emotional Health

*And the peace of God, which surpasses every thought, will guard your hearts and your minds in Christ Jesus. Finally brothers, whatever is true, whatever is honorable, whatever is just, whatever is pure, whatever is lovely, whatever is commendable—if there is any moral excellence and if there is any praise—dwell on these things.*

Philippians 4:7-8 HCSB

Emotional health isn't simply the absence of sadness; it's also the ability to enjoy life and the wisdom to celebrate God's gifts. Christians have every reason to be optimistic about life. As John Calvin observed, "There is not one blade of grass, there is no color in this world that is not intended to make us rejoice." But sometimes, when we are tired or frustrated, rejoicing seems only a distant promise. Thankfully, God stands ready to restore us: "I will give you a new heart and put a new spirit in you..." (Ezekiel 36:26 NIV). Our task, of course, is to let Him.

If you're feeling deeply discouraged or profoundly depressed, then it is time to seriously address the state of your emotional health. First, open your heart to God in prayer. Then, talk with trusted family members, friends, and your pastor. And, if you or someone close to you considers it wise, seek advice from your physician or make an appointment with a licensed mental health professional.

When your emotional health is at stake, you should avail yourself of every reasonable resource. Then, armed with the promises of your Creator and the support of family and friends, you can go about the business of solving the challenges that confront you. When you do, the clouds will eventually part, and the sun will shine once more upon your soul.

### Remember This:

When negative emotions threaten to hijack your day, lift your thoughts—and your prayers—to God.

## More from God's Word

*Don't worry about your life, what you will eat or what you will drink; or about your body, what you will wear. Isn't life more than food and the body more than clothing?*

Matthew 6:25 HCSB

*Don't worry about anything, but in everything, through prayer and petition with thanksgiving, let your requests be made known to God.*

Philippians 4:6 HCSB

*Therefore don't worry about tomorrow, because tomorrow will worry about itself. Each day has enough trouble of its own.*

Matthew 6:34 HCSB

*Yea, though I walk through the valley of the shadow of death, I will fear no evil: for thou art with me; thy rod and thy staff they comfort me.*

Psalm 23:4 KJV

*I will be with you when you pass through the waters . . . when you walk through the fire . . . the flame will not burn you. For I the Lord your God, the Holy One of Israel, and your Savior.*

Isaiah 43:2-3 HCSB

## More Thoughts About Emotional Health

The busier we are, the easier it is to worry, the greater the temptation to worry, the greater the need to be alone with God.

*Charles Stanley*

We sometimes fear to bring our troubles to God because we think they must seem small to Him. But, if they are large enough to vex and endanger our welfare, they are large enough to touch His heart of love.

*R. A. Torrey*

Worry does not empty tomorrow of its sorrow; it empties today of its strength.

*Corrie ten Boom*

## Weight Loss Made Simple

It's really very simple: to lose weight, expend more energy and take in fewer calories. To gain weight, do the opposite. The cure for obesity is simple, but implementing that cure isn't. Weight loss requires lots of planning and lots of self-discipline. But with God's help, you're up to the task.

The spiritual life is a life beyond moods. It is a life in which we choose joy and do not allow ourselves to become victims of passing feelings of happiness or depression.

—

Henri Nouwen

# Sadness Versus Depression

It's been said, and with good reason, that depression is the common cold of mental illness. Why? Because depression is such a common malady. But make no mistake: depression is a serious condition that, if untreated, can take a terrible toll on individuals and families alike.

The sadness that accompanies any significant loss is an inevitable fact of life. In time, sadness runs its course and gradually abates. Depression, on the other hand, is a physical and emotional condition that is, in almost all cases, treatable with medication and counseling. Depression is not a disease to be taken lightly. Left untreated, it presents real dangers to patients' physical health and to their emotional well-being.

If you find yourself feeling "blue," perhaps it's a logical reaction to the ups and downs of daily life. But if your feelings of sadness have gone on longer than you think they should—or if someone close to you fears that your sadness may have evolved into clinical depression—it's time to seek professional help. Consider the following:

1. If you have persistent urges toward self-destructive behavior, or if you feel as though you have lost the will to live, consult a professional counselor or physician immediately.

2. If someone you trust urges you to seek counseling, schedule a session with a professionally trained counselor to evaluate your condition.

3. If you experience persistent and prolonged changes in sleep patterns, or if you experience a significant change in weight (either gain or loss), consult your physician.

4. If you are plagued by consistent, prolonged, severe feelings of hopelessness, consult a physician or professional counselor.

In summary, depression is a serious but treatable condition. If you suspect that depression may have a grip on you or someone you love, seek professional guidance without delay.

### Walk More, Ride Less

In earlier times, our forefathers (and mothers) walked a lot. In these times, we walk a little. Our ancestors had it right—walking is healthy, and most of us should walk much more than we do. It's good for the body as well as the soul.

# Building Healthy Relationships

Emotional health is contagious, and so is emotional distress. If you're fortunate enough to be surrounded by family members and friends who celebrate life and praise God, consider yourself profoundly blessed. But, if you find yourself caught in an unhealthy relationship, it's time to look realistically at your situation and begin making changes.

Don't worry about changing other people: you can't do it. What you can do is to conduct yourself in a responsible fashion and insist that other people treat you with the dignity and consideration that you deserve.

In a perfect world filled with perfect people, our relationships, too, would be perfect. But none of us are perfect and neither are our relationships . . . and that's okay. As we work to make our imperfect relationships a little happier and healthier, we grow as individuals and as families. But, if we find ourselves in relationships that are debilitating or dangerous, then changes must be made, and soon.

If you find yourself caught up in a personal relationship that is bringing havoc into your life, and if you can't seem to find the courage to do something about it, don't hesitate to consult your pastor. Or, you may seek the advice of a trusted friend or a professionally trained counselor. But whatever you do, don't be satisfied with the status quo.

God has grand plans for your life; He has promised you the joy and abundance that can be yours through Him. But to fully experience God's gifts, you need happy, emotionally healthy people to share them with. It's up to you to make sure that you do your part to build the kinds of relationships that will help you experience God's wonderful gifts.

## Controllable Worries About Uncontrollable Problems

Assiduously divide your areas of concern into two categories: those you can control and those you cannot. Then, do your best to refrain from wasting time or energy worrying about the latter.

## More from God's Word About
## the Direction of Your Thoughts

*Set your minds on what is above, not on what is on the earth.*

Colossians 3:2 HCSB

*Brothers, don't be childish in your thinking, but be infants in evil and adult in your thinking.*

1 Corinthians 14:20 HCSB

*Guard your heart above all else, for it is the source of life.*

Proverbs 4:23 HCSB

*May the words of my mouth and the meditation of my heart be acceptable to You, Lord, my rock and my Redeemer.*

Psalm 19:14 HCSB

*Commit your works to the Lord, and your thoughts will be established.*

Proverbs 16:3 NKJV

## Notes to Yourself

In the space below, write down at least three things you can do this week to improve the state of your spiritual health.

_____

_____

_____

_____

_____

_____

_____

_____

_____

_____

_____

_____

_____

# When You Put God First, Good Things Happen

*But seek ye first the kingdom of God, and his righteousness;*
*and all these things shall be added unto you.*

Matthew 6:33 KJV

One of the surest ways to improve your health and your life—and the best way—is to do it with God as your partner. When you put God first in every aspect of your life, you'll be comforted by the knowledge that His wisdom is the ultimate wisdom and that His plans are the right plans for you. When you put God first, your outlook will change, your priorities will change, your behaviors will change, and your health will change. When you put Him first, you'll experience the genuine peace and lasting comfort that only He can give.

In the book of Exodus, God instructs us to place no gods before Him (20:3). Does God rule your heart? Make certain that the honest answer to this question is a resounding yes. And then prepare yourself for the cascade of spiritual and emotional blessings that are sure to follow.

### Remember This:
God deserves first place in your life . . . and you deserve the experience of putting Him there.

## More from God's Word

*The Lord is my strength and my song; He has become my salvation.*

Exodus 15:2 HCSB

*Be careful not to forget the Lord.*

Deuteronomy 6:12 HCSB

*It is good to give thanks to the Lord, and to sing praises to Your name, O Most High; to declare Your lovingkindness in the morning, and Your faithfulness every night.*

Psalm 92:1-2 NKJV

*Love the Lord your God with all your heart, with all your soul, and with all your strength.*

Deuteronomy 6:5 HCSB

*The Devil said to Him, "I will give You their splendor and all this authority, because it has been given over to me, and I can give it to anyone I want. If You, then, will worship me, all will be Yours." And Jesus answered him, "It is written: You shall worship the Lord your God, and Him alone you shall serve."*

Luke 4:6-8 HCSB

## More Thoughts About Putting God First

Make God's will the focus of your life day by day. If you seek to please Him and Him alone, you'll find yourself satisfied with life.

*Kay Arthur*

Jesus Christ is the first and last, author and finisher, beginning and end, alpha and omega, and by Him all other things hold together. He must be first or nothing. God never comes next!

*Vance Havner*

A man's spiritual health is exactly proportional to his love for God.

*C. S. Lewis*

Our body is a portable sanctuary through which we are daily experiencing the presence of God.

*Richard Foster*

## Your Diet Reflects Your Values

If you place a high value on the body God has given you, then you must place high importance on the foods you use to fuel it.

# Perfection Is Impossible

You don't have to be perfect to be wonderful. The difference between perfectionism and realistic expectations is the difference between a life of frustration and a life of contentment. Only one earthly being ever lived life to perfection, and He was the Son of God. The rest of us have fallen short of God's standard and need to be accepting of our own limitations as well as the limitations of others.

If you find yourself frustrated by the unrealistic demands of others (or by unrealistic pressures of the self-imposed variety), it's time to ask yourself who you're trying to impress, and why. Your first responsibility is to the Heavenly Father who created you and to the Son who saved you. Then, you bear a powerful responsibility to be true to yourself. And of course you owe debts of gratitude to friends and family members. But, when it comes to meeting society's unrealistic expectations, forget it! Those expectations aren't just unrealistic; they're detrimental to your spiritual health.

So, if you've become discouraged with your inability to be perfectly fit, remember that when you accepted Christ as your Savior, God accepted you for all eternity. Now, it's your turn to accept yourself. When you do, you'll feel a tremendous weight being lifted from your shoulders. After all, pleasing God is simply a matter of obeying His commandments and accepting His Son. But as for pleasing everybody else? That's impossible . . . so why even try?

**It's Possible to Get Fit and Stay Fit**

Would you like to continue your journey toward improved fitness? Then start with the firm conviction that God wants the very same thing. And then have faith that when you and God work together, anything is possible!

There is no need to fear the decisions of life when you know Jesus Christ, for His name is Counselor.

—

Warren Wiersbe

# Celebrating Life

Today is a non-renewable resource—once it's gone, it's gone forever. Our responsibility, as thoughtful believers, is to use this day in the service of God's will and in the service of His people. When we do so, we enrich our own lives and the lives of those whom we love.

God has richly blessed us, and He wants you to rejoice in His gifts. That's why this day—and each day that follows—should be a time of prayer and celebration as we consider the Good News of God's free gift: salvation through Jesus Christ.

Oswald Chambers correctly observed, "Joy is the great note all throughout the Bible." E. Stanley Jones echoed that thought when he wrote "Christ and joy go together." But, even the most dedicated Christians can, on occasion, forget to celebrate each day for what it is: a priceless gift from God.

What do you expect from the day ahead? Are you expecting God to do wonderful things, or are you living beneath a cloud of apprehension and doubt? The familiar words of Psalm 118:24 remind us of a profound yet simple truth: "This is the day which the LORD hath made" (KJV). Our duty, as believers, is to rejoice in God's marvelous creation.

Today, celebrate the life that God has given you. Today, put a smile on your face, kind words on your lips, and a song in your heart. Be generous with your praise and free with your encouragement. And then, when you have celebrated life to the fullest, invite your friends to do likewise. After all, this is God's day, and He has given us clear instructions for its use. We are commanded to rejoice and be glad. So, with no further ado, let the celebration begin...and never end.

## His Rightful Place

You must guard your heart by putting God in His rightful place—first place.

## More from God's Word About Joy

*Rejoice in the Lord always. I will say it again: Rejoice!*

Philippians 4:4 HCSB

*You will show me the way of life, granting me the joy of your presence and the pleasures of living with you forever.*

Psalm 16:11 NLT

*David and the whole house of Israel were celebrating before the Lord.*

2 Samuel 6:5 HCSB

*Their sorrow was turned into rejoicing and their mourning into a holiday. They were to be days of feasting, rejoicing, and of sending gifts to one another and the poor.*

Esther 9:22 HCSB

*At the dedication of the wall of Jerusalem, they sent for the Levites wherever they lived and brought them to Jerusalem to celebrate the joyous dedication with thanksgiving and singing accompanied by cymbals, harps, and lyres.*

Nehemiah 12:27 HCSB

## Notes to Yourself

Are you putting God first in every aspect of your life? In the space below, describe how you believe God wants you to treat your body.

_____

_____

_____

_____

_____

_____

_____

_____

_____

_____

_____

_____

_____

A wise man will hear
and increase learning,
and a man of understanding
will attain wise counsel.

—

Proverbs 1:5 NKJV

# Read the Bible
# in a Year

# JANUARY

| 1<br>Genesis 1-2<br>Matthew 1 | 2<br>Genesis 3-5<br>Matthew 2 | 3<br>Genesis 6-8<br>Matthew 3 |
|---|---|---|
| 4<br>Genesis 9-11<br>Matthew 4 | 5<br>Genesis 12-14<br>Matthew 5:1-20 | 6<br>Genesis 15-17<br>Matthew 5:21-48 |
| 7<br>Genesis 18-19<br>Matthew 6:1-18 | 8<br>Genesis 20-21<br>Matthew 6:19-34 | 9<br>Genesis 22-25<br>Matthew 7 |
| 10<br>Genesis 26-27<br>Matthew 8:1-20 | 11<br>Genesis 28-29<br>Matthew 8:21-34 | 12<br>Genesis 30-31<br>Matthew 9:1-17 |
| 13<br>Genesis 32-33<br>Matthew 9:18-38 | 14<br>Genesis 34-35<br>Matthew 10:1-24 | 15<br>Genesis 36-38<br>Matthew 10:25-42 |
| 16<br>Genesis 39-40<br>Matthew 11 | 17<br>Genesis 41-42<br>Matthew 12:1-24 | 18<br>Genesis 43-44<br>Matthew 12:25-50 |
| 19<br>Genesis 45-46<br>Matthew 13:1-36 | 20<br>Genesis 47-48<br>Matthew 13:37-58 | 21<br>Genesis 49-50<br>Matthew 14 |
| 22<br>Exodus 1-3<br>Matthew 15:1-20 | 23<br>Exodus 4-6<br>Matthew 15:21-39 | 24<br>Exodus 7-9<br>Matthew 16 |
| 25<br>Exodus 10-12<br>Matthew 17 | 26<br>Exodus 13-14<br>Matthew 18:1-20 | 27<br>Exodus 15-16<br>Matthew 18:21-35 |
| 28<br>Exodus 17-18<br>Matthew 19 | 29<br>Exodus 19-20<br>Matthew 20:1-16 | 30<br>Exodus 21-22<br>Matthew 20:17-34 |
| 31<br>Exodus 23-24<br>Matthew 21:1-22 | | |

# FEBRUARY

| | | |
|---|---|---|
| 1<br>Exodus 25-27<br>Matthew 21:23-46 | 2<br>Exodus 28-30<br>Matthew 22:1-22 | 3<br>Exodus 31-33<br>Matthew 22:23-46 |
| 4<br>Exodus 34-35<br>Matthew 23 | 5<br>Exodus 36-37<br>Matthew 24:1-28 | 6<br>Exodus 38-39<br>Matthew 24:29-51 |
| 7<br>Exodus 40<br>Matthew 25 | 8<br>Leviticus 1-2<br>Matthew 26:1-29 | 9<br>Leviticus 3-4<br>Matthew 26:30-56 |
| 10<br>Leviticus 5-6<br>Matthew 26:57-75 | 11<br>Leviticus 7-8<br>Matthew 27:1-26 | 12<br>Leviticus 9-10<br>Matthew 27:27-53 |
| 13<br>Leviticus 11-12<br>Matthew 27:54-66 | 14<br>Leviticus 13-14<br>Matthew 28 | 15<br>Leviticus 15-16<br>Mark 1:1-28 |
| 16<br>Leviticus 17-18<br>Mark 1:29-45 | 17<br>Leviticus 19-20<br>Mark 2 | 18<br>Leviticus 21-22<br>Mark 3:1-19 |
| 19<br>Leviticus 23-24<br>Mark 3:20-35 | 20<br>Leviticus 25<br>Mark 4:1-20 | 21<br>Leviticus 26-27<br>Mark 4:21-41 |
| 22<br>Numbers 1-2<br>Mark 5:1-19 | 23<br>Numbers 3-4<br>Mark 5:20-43 | 24<br>Numbers 5-6<br>Mark 6:1-12 |
| 25<br>Numbers 7-9<br>Mark 6:13-32 | 26<br>Numbers 10-12<br>Mark 6:33-56 | 27<br>Numbers 13-15<br>Mark 7:1-13 |
| 28<br>Numbers 16-18<br>Mark 7:14-37 | | |
| | | |

# MARCH

| 1<br>Numbers 19-21<br>Mark 8:1-13 | 2<br>Numbers 22-24<br>Mark 8:14-38 | 3<br>Numbers 25-27<br>Mark 9:1-29 |
|---|---|---|
| 4<br>Numbers 28-30<br>Mark 9:30-50 | 5<br>Numbers 31-33<br>Mark 10:1-31 | 6<br>Numbers 34-36<br>Mark 10:32-52 |
| 7<br>Deuteronomy 1-3<br>Mark 11:1-19 | 8<br>Deuteronomy 4-6<br>Mark 11:20-33 | 9<br>Deuteronomy 7-9<br>Mark 12:1-28 |
| 10<br>Deuteronomy 10-12<br>Mark 12:29-44 | 11<br>Deuteronomy 13-15<br>Mark 13 | 12<br>Deuteronomy 16-18<br>Mark 14:1-9 |
| 13<br>Deuteronomy 19-21<br>Mark 14:10-36 | 14<br>Deuteronomy 22-24<br>Mark 14:37-72 | 15<br>Deuteronomy 25-27<br>Mark 15:1-26 |
| 16<br>Deuteronomy 28-30<br>Mark 15:27-47 | 17<br>Deuteronomy 31-32<br>Mark 16 | 18<br>Deuteronomy 33-34<br>Luke 1:1-38 |
| 19<br>Joshua 1-3<br>Luke 1:39-80 | 20<br>Joshua 4-6<br>Luke 2:1-24 | 21<br>Joshua 7-9<br>Luke 2:25-52 |
| 22<br>Joshua 10-12<br>Luke 3:1-18 | 23<br>Joshua 13-15<br>Luke 3:19-38 | 24<br>Joshua 16-18<br>Luke 4:1-13 |
| 25<br>Joshua 19-21<br>Luke 4:14-30 | 26<br>Joshua 22-24<br>Luke 4:31-44 | 27<br>Judges 1-2<br>Luke 5:1-16 |
| 28<br>Judges 3-5<br>Luke 5:17-39 | 29<br>Judges 6-8<br>Luke 6:1-18 | 30<br>Judges 9-11<br>Luke 6:19-49 |
| 31<br>Judges 12-13<br>Luke 7:1-28 | | |

# APRIL

| 1<br>Judges 14-15<br>Luke 7:29-50 | 2<br>Judges 16-17<br>Luke 8:1-21 | 3<br>Judges 18-19<br>Luke 8:22-40 |
|---|---|---|
| 4<br>Judges 20-21<br>Luke 8:41-56 | 5<br>Ruth 1-2<br>Luke 9:1-17 | 6<br>Ruth 3-4<br>Luke 9:18-36 |
| 7<br>1 Samuel 1-3<br>Luke 9:37-62 | 8<br>1 Samuel 4-6<br>Luke 10:1-24 | 9<br>1 Samuel 7-9<br>Luke 10:25-42 |
| 10<br>1 Samuel 10-12<br>Luke 11:1-36 | 11<br>1 Samuel 13-15<br>Luke 11:37-54 | 12<br>1 Samuel 16-18<br>Luke 12:1-40 |
| 13<br>1 Samuel 19-21<br>Luke 12:41-59 | 14<br>1 Samuel 22-24<br>Luke 13:1-21 | 15<br>1 Samuel 25-27<br>Luke 13:22-35 |
| 16<br>1 Samuel 28-29<br>Luke 14:1-14 | 17<br>1 Samuel 30-31<br>Luke 14:15-35 | 18<br>2 Samuel 1-3<br>Luke 15 |
| 19<br>2 Samuel 4-6<br>Luke 16:1-13 | 20<br>2 Samuel 7-9<br>Luke 16:14-31 | 21<br>2 Samuel 10-12<br>Luke 17:1-19 |
| 22<br>2 Samuel 13-15<br>Luke 17:20-37 | 23<br>2 Samuel 16-18<br>Luke 18:1-17 | 24<br>2 Samuel 19-21<br>Luke 18:18-43 |
| 25<br>2 Samuel 22-24<br>Luke 19:1-27 | 26<br>1 Kings 1-2<br>Luke 19:28-48 | 27<br>1 Kings 3-4<br>Luke 20:1-18 |
| 28<br>1 Kings 5-6<br>Luke 20:19-47 | 29<br>1 Kings 7-8<br>Luke 21 | 30<br>1 Kings 9-10<br>Luke 22:1-22 |
|  |  |  |

# MAY

| 1<br>1 Kings 11-12<br>Luke 22:23-53 | 2<br>1 Kings 13-14<br>Luke 22:54-71 | 3<br>1 Kings 15-16<br>Luke 23:1-25 |
|---|---|---|
| 4<br>1 Kings 17-18<br>Luke 23:26-56 | 5<br>1 Kings 19-20<br>Luke 24:1-20 | 6<br>1 Kings 21-22<br>Luke 24:21-36 |
| 7<br>2 Kings 1-2<br>Luke 24:37-53 | 8<br>2 Kings 3-5<br>John 1:1-28 | 9<br>2 Kings 6-8<br>John 1:29-51 |
| 10<br>2 Kings 9-11<br>John 2 | 11<br>2 Kings 12-13<br>John 3:1-21 | 12<br>2 Kings 14-16<br>John 3:22-36 |
| 13<br>2 Kings 17-19<br>John 4:1-30 | 14<br>2 Kings 20-21<br>John 4:31-54 | 15<br>2 Kings 22-23<br>John 5:1-18 |
| 16<br>2 Kings 24-25<br>John 5:19-47 | 17<br>1 Chronicles 1-3<br>John 6:1-21 | 18<br>1 Chronicles 4-6<br>John 6:22-40 |
| 19<br>1 Chronicles 7-9<br>John 6:41-58 | 20<br>1 Chronicles 10-12<br>John 6:59-71 | 21<br>1 Chronicles 13-15<br>John 7:1-32 |
| 22<br>1 Chronicles 16-18<br>John 7:33-53 | 23<br>1 Chronicles 19-21<br>John 8:1-30 | 24<br>1 Chronicles 22-24<br>John 8:31-59 |
| 25<br>1 Chronicles 25-26<br>John 9 | 26<br>1 Chronicles 27-29<br>John 10:1-18 | 27<br>2 Chronicles 1-2<br>John 10:19-42 |
| 28<br>2 Chronicles 3-5<br>John 11:1-29 | 29<br>2 Chronicles 6-8<br>John 11:30-57 | 30<br>2 Chronicles 9-11<br>John 12:1-16 |
| 31<br>2 Chronicles 12-14<br>John 12:17-36 | | |

# JUNE

| 1<br>2 Chronicles 15-17<br>John 12:37-50 | 2<br>2 Chronicles 18-19<br>John 13:1-20 | 3<br>2 Chronicles 20-21<br>John 13:21-38 |
|---|---|---|
| 4<br>2 Chronicles 22-23<br>John 14 | 5<br>2 Chronicles 24-25<br>John 15 | 6<br>2 Chronicles 26-27<br>John 16 |
| 7<br>2 Chronicles 28-29<br>John 17 | 8<br>2 Chronicles 30-31<br>John 18:1-19 | 9<br>2 Chronicles 32-34<br>John 18:20-40 |
| 10<br>2 Chronicles 35-36<br>John 19:1-28 | 11<br>Ezra 1-3<br>John 19:29-42 | 12<br>Ezra 4-6<br>John 20 |
| 13<br>Ezra 7-8<br>John 21 | 14<br>Ezra 9-10<br>Acts 1 | 15<br>Nehemiah 1-2<br>Acts 2 |
| 16<br>Nehemiah 3-5<br>Acts 3 | 17<br>Nehemiah 6-8<br>Acts 4 | 18<br>Nehemiah 9-10<br>Acts 5 |
| 19<br>Nehemiah 11-13<br>Acts 6 | 20<br>Esther 1-3<br>Acts 7:1-39 | 21<br>Esther 4-5<br>Acts 7:40-60 |
| 22<br>Esther 6-7<br>Acts 8:1-13 | 23<br>Esther 8-10<br>Acts 8:14-40 | 24<br>Job 1-3<br>Acts 9:1-22 |
| 25<br>Job 4-5<br>Acts 9:23-43 | 26<br>Job 6-7<br>Acts 10:1-23 | 27<br>Job 8-9<br>Acts 10:24-48 |
| 28<br>Job 10-11<br>Acts 11:1-18 | 29<br>Job 12-14<br>Acts 11:19-30 | 30<br>Job 15-17<br>Acts 12 |

# JULY

| | | |
|---|---|---|
| 1<br>Job 18-20<br>Acts 13:1-12 | 2<br>Job 21-23<br>Acts 13:13-31 | 3<br>Job 24-26<br>Acts 13:32-52 |
| 4<br>Job 27-29<br>Acts 14 | 5<br>Job 30-32<br>Acts 15:1-21 | 6<br>Job 33-34<br>Acts 15:22-41 |
| 7<br>Job 35-36<br>Acts 16:1-22 | 8<br>Job 37-38<br>Acts 16:23-40 | 9<br>Job 39-40<br>Acts 17:1-15 |
| 10<br>Job 41-42<br>Acts 17:16-34 | 11<br>Psalms 1-3<br>Acts 18 | 12<br>Psalms 4-6<br>Acts 19 |
| 13<br>Psalms 7-8<br>Acts 20 | 14<br>Psalms 9-11<br>Acts 21:1-17 | 15<br>Psalms 12-14<br>Acts 21:18-40 |
| 16<br>Psalms 15-17<br>Acts 22:1-11 | 17<br>Psalms 18<br>Acts 22:12-30 | 18<br>Psalms 19-20<br>Acts 23:1-11 |
| 19<br>Psalms 21-22<br>Acts 23:12-35 | 20<br>Psalms 23-25<br>Acts 24 | 21<br>Psalms 26-27<br>Acts 25 |
| 22<br>Psalms 28-29<br>Acts 26 | 23<br>Psalms 30-33<br>Acts 27:1-18 | 24<br>Psalms 34-35<br>Acts 27:19-44 |
| 25<br>Psalms 36-38<br>Acts 28:1-10 | 26<br>Psalms 39-41<br>Acts 28:11-31 | 27<br>Psalms 42-44<br>Romans 1 |
| 28<br>Psalms 45-46<br>Romans 2 | 29<br>Psalms 47-48<br>Romans 3 | 30<br>Psalms 49-50<br>Romans 4 |
| 31<br>Psalms 51-53<br>Romans 5 | | |

# AUGUST

| 1<br>Psalms 54-57<br>Romans 6 | 2<br>Psalms 58-60<br>Romans 7 | 3<br>Psalms 61-64<br>Romans 8:1-21 |
|---|---|---|
| 4<br>Psalms 65-66<br>Romans 8:22-39 | 5<br>Psalms 67-68<br>Romans 9:1-16 | 6<br>Psalms 69<br>Romans 9:17-33 |
| 7<br>Psalms 70-72<br>Romans 10 | 8<br>Psalms 73-74<br>Romans 11:1-21 | 9<br>Psalms 75-77<br>Romans 11:22-36 |
| 10<br>Psalms 78<br>Romans 12 | 11<br>Psalms 79-81<br>Romans 13 | 12<br>Psalms 82-85<br>Romans 14 |
| 13<br>Psalms 86-88<br>Romans 15:1-13 | 14<br>Psalms 89<br>Romans 15:14-21 | 15<br>Psalms 90-93<br>Romans 15:22-33 |
| 16<br>Psalms 94-97<br>Romans 16 | 17<br>Psalms 98-100<br>1 Corinthians 1 | 18<br>Psalms 101-103<br>1 Corinthians 2 |
| 19<br>Psalms 104-105<br>1 Corinthians 3 | 20<br>Psalms 106<br>1 Corinthians 4 | 21<br>Psalms 107-109<br>1 Corinthians 5 |
| 22<br>Psalms 110-113<br>1 Corinthians 6 | 23<br>Psalms 114-118<br>1 Corinthians 7 | 24<br>Psalms 119:1-72<br>1 Corinthians 8 |
| 25<br>Psalms 119:73-176<br>1 Corinthians 9 | 26<br>Psalms 120-123<br>1 Corinthians 10:1-13 | 27<br>Psalms 124-127<br>1 Corinthians 10:14-33 |
| 28<br>Psalms 128-132<br>1 Corinthians 11:1-18 | 29<br>Psalms 133-135<br>1 Corinthians 11:19-34 | 30<br>Psalms 136-138<br>1 Corinthians 12:1-18 |
| 31<br>Psalms 139<br>1 Corinthians 12:19-31 | | |

# SEPTEMBER

| | | |
|---|---|---|
| 1<br>Psalms 140-142<br>1 Corinthians 13 | 2<br>Psalms 143-145<br>1 Corinthians 14:1-19 | 3<br>Psalms 146-147<br>1 Corinthians 14:20-40 |
| 4<br>Psalms 148-150<br>1 Corinthians 15:1-11 | 5<br>Proverbs 1<br>1 Corinthians 15:12-25 | 6<br>Proverbs 2-3<br>1 Corinthians 15:26-58 |
| 7<br>Proverbs 4-5<br>1 Corinthians 16 | 8<br>Proverbs 6-7<br>2 Corinthians 1 | 9<br>Proverbs 8-9<br>2 Corinthians 2 |
| 10<br>Proverbs 10-11<br>2 Corinthians 3 | 11<br>Proverbs 12-13<br>2 Corinthians 4 | 12<br>Proverbs 14-15<br>2 Corinthians 5 |
| 13<br>Proverbs 16-17<br>2 Corinthians 6 | 14<br>Proverbs 18-19<br>2 Corinthians 7-8 | 15<br>Proverbs 20-21<br>2 Corinthians 9 |
| 16<br>Proverbs 22-23<br>2 Corinthians 10 | 17<br>Proverbs 24-25<br>2 Corinthians 11:1-11 | 18<br>Proverbs 26-27<br>2 Corinthians 11:12-33 |
| 19<br>Proverbs 28-29<br>2 Corinthians 12 | 20<br>Proverbs 30-31<br>2 Corinthians 13 | 21<br>Ecclesiastes 1-3<br>Galatians 1 |
| 22<br>Ecclesiastes 4-6<br>Galatians 2 | 23<br>Ecclesiastes 7-8<br>Galatians 3 | 24<br>Ecclesiastes 9-12<br>Galatians 4 |
| 25<br>Song of Solomon 1-4<br>Galatians 5 | 26<br>Song of Solomon 5-8<br>Galatians 6 | 27<br>Isaiah 1-2<br>Ephesians 1 |
| 28<br>Isaiah 3-4<br>Ephesians 2 | 29<br>Isaiah 5-6<br>Ephesians 3 | 30<br>Isaiah 7-8<br>Ephesians 4 |
| | | |

# OCTOBER

| 1<br>Isaiah 9-10<br>Ephesians 5 | 2<br>Isaiah 11-12<br>Ephesians 6 | 3<br>Isaiah 13-14<br>Philippians 1 |
|---|---|---|
| 4<br>Isaiah 15-16<br>Philippians 2 | 5<br>Isaiah 17-19<br>Philippians 3 | 6<br>Isaiah 20-22<br>Philippians 4 |
| 7<br>Isaiah 23-25<br>Colossians 1 | 8<br>Isaiah 26-27<br>Colossians 2 | 9<br>Isaiah 28-29<br>Colossians 3 |
| 10<br>Isaiah 30-31<br>Colossians 4 | 11<br>Isaiah 32-33<br>1 Thessalonians 1 | 12<br>Isaiah 34-35<br>1 Thessalonians 2 |
| 13<br>Isaiah 36-37<br>1 Thessalonians 3 | 14<br>Isaiah 38-39<br>1 Thessalonians 4 | 15<br>Isaiah 40-42<br>1 Thessalonians 5 |
| 16<br>Isaiah 43-45<br>2 Thessalonians 1 | 17<br>Isaiah 46-48<br>2 Thessalonians 2 | 18<br>Isaiah 49-51<br>2 Thessalonians 3 |
| 19<br>Isaiah 52-54<br>1 Timothy 1 | 20<br>Isaiah 55-57<br>1 Timothy 2 | 21<br>Isaiah 58-60<br>1 Timothy 3 |
| 22<br>Isaiah 61-63<br>1 Timothy 4 | 23<br>Isaiah 64-66<br>1 Timothy 5 | 24<br>Jeremiah 1-3<br>1 Timothy 6 |
| 25<br>Jeremiah 4-6<br>2 Timothy 1 | 26<br>Jeremiah 7-9<br>2 Timothy 2 | 27<br>Jeremiah 10-12<br>2 Timothy 3 |
| 28<br>Jeremiah 13-15<br>2 Timothy 4 | 29<br>Jeremiah 16-18<br>Titus 1 | 30<br>Jeremiah 19-20<br>Titus 2 |
| 31<br>Jeremiah 21-22<br>Titus 3 | | |

# NOVEMBER

| 1 Jeremiah 23-24 Philemon | 2 Jeremiah 25-27 Hebrews 1 | 3 Jeremiah 28-30 Hebrews 2 |
|---|---|---|
| 4 Jeremiah 31-32 Hebrews 3 | 5 Jeremiah 33-35 Hebrews 4 | 6 Jeremiah 36-38 Hebrews 5 |
| 7 Jeremiah 39-41 Hebrews 6 | 8 Jeremiah 42-44 Hebrews 7 | 9 Jeremiah 45-47 Hebrews 8 |
| 10 Jeremiah 48-49 Hebrews 9 | 11 Jeremiah 50 Hebrews 10:1-22 | 12 Jeremiah 51 Hebrews 10:23-39 |
| 13 Jeremiah 52 Hebrews 11:1-16 | 14 Lamentations 1-2 Hebrews 11:17-40 | 15 Lamentations 3-5 Hebrews 12:1-13 |
| 16 Ezekiel 1-2 Hebrews 12:14-29 | 17 Ezekiel 3-5 Hebrews 13 | 18 Ezekiel 6-7 James 1 |
| 19 Ezekiel 8-10 James 2 | 20 Ezekiel 11-13 James 3 | 21 Ezekiel 14-16 James 4 |
| 22 Ezekiel 17-18 James 5 | 23 Ezekiel 19-20 1 Peter 1 | 24 Ezekiel 21-22 1 Peter 2 |
| 25 Ezekiel 23-24 1 Peter 3 | 26 Ezekiel 25-27 1 Peter 4 | 27 Ezekiel 28-30 1 Peter 5 |
| 28 Ezekiel 31-33 2 Peter 1 | 29 Ezekiel 34-36 2 Peter 2 | 30 Ezekiel 37-39 2 Peter 3 |

# DECEMBER

| 1<br>Ezekiel 40-41<br>1 John 1 | 2<br>Ezekiel 42-44<br>1 John 2 | 3<br>Ezekiel 45-46<br>1 John 3 |
|---|---|---|
| 4<br>Ezekiel 47-48<br>1 John 4 | 5<br>Daniel 1-2<br>1 John 5 | 6<br>Daniel 3-4<br>2 John |
| 7<br>Daniel 5-6<br>3 John | 8<br>Daniel 7-8<br>Jude | 9<br>Daniel 9-10<br>Revelation 1 |
| 10<br>Daniel 11-12<br>Revelation 2 | 11<br>Hosea 1-3<br>Revelation 3 | 12<br>Hosea 4-7<br>Revelation 4 |
| 13<br>Hosea 8-11<br>Revelation 5 | 14<br>Hosea 12-14<br>Revelation 6 | 15<br>Joel 1-3<br>Revelation 7 |
| 16<br>Amos 1-4<br>Revelation 8 | 17<br>Amos 5-9<br>Revelation 9 | 18<br>Obadiah<br>Revelation 10 |
| 19<br>Jonah 1-4<br>Revelation 11 | 20<br>Micah 1-3<br>Revelation 12 | 21<br>Micah 4-5<br>Revelation 13 |
| 22<br>Micah 6-7<br>Revelation 14 | 23<br>Nahum 1-3<br>Revelation 15 | 24<br>Habakkuk 1-3<br>Revelation 16 |
| 25<br>Zephaniah 1-3<br>Revelation 17 | 26<br>Haggai 1-2<br>Revelation 18 | 27<br>Zechariah 1-4<br>Revelation 19 |
| 28<br>Zechariah 5-8<br>Revelation 20 | 29<br>Zechariah 9-11<br>Revelation 21 | 30<br>Zechariah 12-14<br>Revelation 22:1-8 |
| 31<br>Malachi 1-4<br>Revelation 22:9-21 | | |